AMERICAN BIBLE SOCIETY

FAVORITE BIBLE STORIES AND AMAZING FACTS

Publisher: Richard Fraiman
General Manager: Steven Sandonato
Executive Director, Marketing Services: Carol Pittard
Executive Director, Retail & Special Sales: Tom Mifsud
Executive Director, New Product Development: Peter Harper
Editorial Director: Steve Koepp
Director, Bookazine Development & Marketing: Laura Adam
Publishing Director: Joy Butts
Assistant General Counsel: Helen Wan
Book Production Manager: Susan Chodakiewicz
Design & Prepress Manager: Anne-Michelle Gallero
Brand Manager, Product Marketing: Nina Fleishman
Associate Prepress Manager: Alex Voznesenskiy

Special Thanks to:

- Victoria Alfonso
- Christine Austin
- Jeremy Biloon
- Glenn Buonocore
- Malati Chavali
- Jim Childs
- Rose Cirrincione
- Jacqueline Fitzgerald
- Carrie Hertan
- Christine Font
- Lauren Hall
- Suzanne Janso
- Malena Jones
- Mona Li
- Robert Marasco
- Kimberly Marshall
- Amy Migliaccio
- Nina Mistry
- Dave Rozzelle
- Ilene Schreider
- Adriana Tierno
- Vanessa Wu

Consulting Editors from American Bible Society's
Nida Institute for Biblical Scholarship:

Thomas R. May
Davina C. McDonald
Philip H. Towner, Ph.D.

**With special thanks to American Bible Society's
Committee on Translation and Scholarship**

Q2AMEDIA
Engage • Enrich • Empower

Created by **Q2A Media**
Editor: Eva Moore
Project Manager: Arushi Chawla
Art Director: Suzan Kadribasic
Designer: Kanika Kohli
Illustrators: Ishan Varma and Vikash Gurung

ISBN 10: 1-60320-933-6
ISBN 13: 978-1-60320-933-5

We welcome your comments and suggestions about Time Home Entertainment Inc. Books. Please write to us at:
Time Home Entertainment Inc. Books
Attention: Book Editors
PO Box 11016
Des Moines, IA 50336-1016

If you would like to order any of our hardcover Collector's Edition books, please call us at 1-800-327-6388.
(Monday through Friday, 7:00 a.m.—8:00 p.m. or Saturday, 7:00 a.m.—6:00 p.m. Central Time).
1 QGT 11

Welcome to an unforgettable adventure

Did you know that the Bible is one of the most exciting books of all time? In the Bible, you can find stories rife with adventure, danger, disasters, miracles, heroes and villains, warriors and peacemakers, joy and sorrow. This book presents 27 of these timeless tales, selected especially for young readers and listeners. Retold in simple, contemporary text with illustrations that capture the action, beauty, and drama of the tales, the book covers a wide range of topics suitable for the entire family. Each story may serve as a springboard for family devotions and discussions about biblical truths, or may be approached as independent leisure reading.

Through dramatic dialogue and vivid imagery, readers will find themselves vicariously experiencing the devastation of the Flood with its ending message of hope; the dramatic story of Joseph and his brothers; David's victory over the giant, Goliath, and Daniel's fearful encounter with death in the lion's den; Esther's courage in saving her people from the plot of a jealous enemy; the joy of the birth of Jesus and the many miracles he performed, and much more. In all of the stories the Word of God, based mainly on American Bible Society's *Contemporary English Version* of the Bible, speaks forcefully to both adult and child.

Reflection questions appear at the end of each story and challenge young readers to reason beyond the literal level, thus thinking on critical and life-application levels. Children grasp, for example, that it is not only important to recall what happens between Joseph and his brothers, but also to decipher the "whys" of their actions. And to further enhance the child's reading pleasure, each story is followed by "amazing facts"— eye-catching pages with tidbits of religious, geographical and cultural information that enhance and expand the content of the story.

The amazing world of the Bible is at your fingertips; all you need to do is turn the pages.

Old Testament Stories

New Testament Stories

How do you say that?

Some of the names in the Bible look strange to us.
This is how to say the names:

Key

Short vowel sounds	Long vowel sounds
• AH – 'a' sound	• AY – 'a' sound
• EH – 'e' sound	• EE - 'e' sound
• IH – 'i' sound	• IE – 'i' sound
• OH – 'o' sound	• OOH – 'o' sound
• UH – 'u' sound	• UUH – 'u' sound

THE STORY OF ABRAHAM
JOSEPH   IN EGYPT
| Sarai | **SAY**-rie |
| Shechem | **SHEH**-kem |

THE STORY OF MOSES
| Jochabed | **JOK**-eh-bed |
| Midian | **MID**-ee-an |

THE EXODUS
| Succoth | **SUC**-coth |

THE STORY OF SAMSON
| Philistines | fil-**IS**-tinz |

THE STORY OF RUTH
| Elimelech | eh-**LIM**-eh-leck |

DAVID AND GOLIATH
Eliab	ee-**LIE**-ab
Abinadab	ah-**BIN**-ah-dab
Shammah	**SHAM**-mah

THE COURAGE OF ESTHER
| Xeres | **ZERK**-cees |
| Amalekites | ah-**MAL**-ek-ites |

JONAH AND THE FISH
| Nineveh | **NIN**-eh-vah |
| Ninevites | **NIN**-eh-vites |

DANIEL IN THE LIONS' DEN
| Nebuchadnezzar | Neb-uuh-cad-**NEZ**-zer |
| Babylonia | bab-ih-**LOOH**-nee-ah |

JESUS THE HEALER
| Capernaum | kah-**PER**-nee-um |
| Bartimaeus | bar-tih-**MAY**-us |

JESUS CHOOSES TWELVE
Zebedee	**ZEB**-eh-dee
Alphaeus	Al-**FEE**-us
Thaddaeus	Thad-**DEE**-us
Iscariot	is-**CAHR**-ee-ott
Tyre	**TIRE**
Sidon	**SIE**-don

THE EASTER STORY
Pontius Pilate	**PON**-she-us **PIE**-lut
Gethsemane	geth-**SEM**-ah-nee
Barabbas	bah-**RAHB**-as
Golgotha	**GOHL**-goh-thah

Old Testament Stories

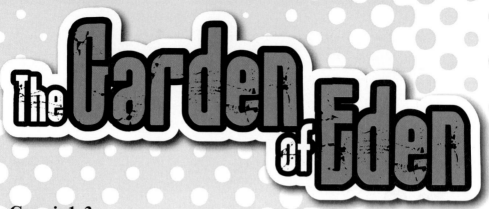
The Garden of Eden

Genesis 1–3

God creates the earth, the animals, and the first people—Adam and Eve.

In the beginning God created the heavens and the earth, but darkness was all around. God said, "I command light to shine!" And light began to shine. God named the light "Day" and the darkness "Night." Evening came and then morning—that was the first day.

Then, God made a dome to separate the water above from the water below. He called the dome "Sky." That was the work God did on the second day.

There was nothing but water under the sky. God said, "I command the water to come together in one place, so there will be dry ground." He called the water "Ocean," and he called the dry parts "Land."

Next, God commanded the land to produce all kinds of plants, including fruit trees, fields of grain, flowers, herbs, and vines. God looked at all he had done on the third day, and it was good.

On the fourth day, God created the sun to rule the day and the moon to rule the night. God also set stars in the sky. Now there was day and night, spring, summer, fall, and winter. It was good.

On the fifth day, God said, "I command the ocean to be full of living creatures," and there appeared the octopuses, whales, sharks, trout, salmon, starfish, and every other kind of animal that lives in the sea.

But God had more to do. "I command birds to fly above the earth," he said. All kinds of birds appeared: eagles, owls, sparrows, hummingbirds, pelicans, bluebirds, falcons, and every other kind of bird.

God told the fish and the birds to live everywhere and fill up the earth with their offspring. And it was good.

There were still no land animals, though. So, on the sixth day, God said, "I command the earth to give life to all kinds of tame animals, wild animals, and reptiles."

Now the land was full of animals of all sizes and shapes—elephants to caterpillars, gorillas to inchworms. It was good, but something was missing. So God took some soil from the ground and made a man. God called him Adam and breathed life into him.

God looked at all he had made. It was very good!

By the seventh day, he was done. God blessed the seventh day and made it special because on that day he rested from his work.

The Garden of Eden

During the first six days, God prepared a garden in a place called Eden. It was filled with beautiful plants and fruit trees. God put Adam in the garden and told him to take care of it.

God took Adam to see a very special tree that was growing right in the middle of the garden. He said, "Adam, you may eat the fruit of any tree except this one."

Adam said, "The fruit on this tree looks so good. Why can't I eat some?"

"This fruit gives the power to know the difference between right and wrong. That knowledge is not for man, only for God. If you eat this fruit, something terrible will happen to you."

God didn't want Adam to live alone in the garden, so he placed some animals and birds in the garden to keep Adam company. God asked Adam to name every creature: the tame animals, the wild animals, and the birds. That's how they got their names.

Adam liked living with the animals, but God saw that none of them was the right partner for Adam. So one night, when Adam was in a deep sleep, God took a rib from Adam and made a woman.

Now Adam was happy. "Here is someone who is like me!" he said.

Adam named the woman, Eve.

Now everything was perfect in the Garden of Eden!

The Snake

One day, Eve was sitting under the special tree in the middle of the garden. A snake was resting on its branches. Now, this snake was sneaky and mean and he was up to no good.

"Eve," he said, "do you eat the fruit of all the trees-s-s-s in the garden?"

Eve replied, "Yes," she said. Then, "Oh, wait. God told us not to eat the fruit growing on this tree. If we do, something terrible will happen."

"Don't be s-s-s-silly," the snake said. "All that will happen is-s-s-s that you will know the difference between right and wrong, just as God does."

Eve looked at the fruit. She liked the idea of knowing something special. Besides, the fruit looked delicious. She reached up and picked one. She took a bite.

Just as Eve was about to take another bite, Adam came by.

"Here, try some," Eve said, holding her hand out. "It's really good."

Adam looked at the fruit, and he couldn't resist tasting it.

Suddenly, Adam and Eve knew something had changed. They saw that they were different from each other. They felt so ashamed that they sewed together some leaves from the fig tree to cover themselves.

Then they heard God walking in the garden. They hid behind some bushes.

God was looking for Adam. "Where are you?" he called.

But God knew very well where Adam was. "Did you eat any fruit from the tree in the middle of the garden?"

Adam peeked out from behind the bush. "Eve took some and gave it to me, and I ate it."

God asked the woman, "What have you done?"

The woman answered, "It was the snake. It tricked me."

God was very angry. He told the snake that as its punishment—it would forever after crawl on its stomach and eat dirt.

Think about it...

If Adam and Eve weren't supposed to eat from the tree of knowledge, why do you think God put it in the garden?

But for Adam and Eve, the punishment was much worse.

"You must leave the Garden of Eden. You will have to work to grow your own food, and you will suffer much pain. Life will be very different, and very hard."

God gave Adam and Eve clothes made of animal skins. The man and woman walked sadly out to the land beyond the garden. God placed angels to guard the entrance so that they could never return.

All About the Garden of Eden

So where was the Garden of Eden?

The Bible says that God made the garden where "a river flowed from Eden and divided into four rivers—the Pishon, Gihon, Tigris and Euphrates." No one today is sure of where the Pishon and Gihon Rivers might have been, but we know about the Tigris and the Euphrates. They begin in Turkey and flow through Iraq. (The Euphrates River also crosses Syria.) So some people believe the garden could have been located in what is now the country of Turkey, but so far, no one has been able to prove it.

The Sneaky Serpent

Ever since the Garden of Eden, snakes have had a bad rap. It was once believed that all snakes were poisonous, so people were afraid of them. Even in the time of Jesus, wicked or dishonest people were called snakes, or vipers. We say that someone "speaks with a forked tongue" when they are not telling the truth. This expression refers to the shape of a snake's tongue. Today, we know that there are all kinds of snakes in the world and that many are harmless and make good pets.

The lump that sticks out of the human throat, especially in boys and men, is called an "Adam's apple" because it looks like it was caused by the fruit sticking in Adam's throat as he swallowed.

YOU CAN'T HAVE IT!

When your parents forbid you to do something, it means you do not have their permission. God did not give Adam permission to eat the fruit of the special tree, so the fruit was forbidden to him. The expression "forbidden fruit" has come to mean anything that a person really, really wants but shouldn't have.

In the Hebrew language, the word for "man" and "Adam" are the same. Adam named his wife "Eve," the Hebrew word for "living," because she would be the mother of all people who live.

But was it really an apple?

The Bible never says that the fruit Adam and Eve ate was an apple. Some experts say it could have been some other fruit, such as a grape, a fig (based on the account of Adam and Eve using fig leaves to cover themselves), a pomegranate, a tomato (a fruit!), or a pear.

The Story of Noah

Genesis 6–9

After Adam and Eve, more and more people were born. Now there are millions of men and women, just as God had wanted. But these people have become violent and cruel. God can find only one good man on earth—Noah.

Noah stared up at the dark clouds gathering in the sky. Then he looked at the mass of animals gathered around the huge boat that he and his sons had built.

There were animals that walked and animals that flew. There were creatures that crawled and others that slithered along the ground. Noah could barely hear above the roars and yelps and snorts.

Noah called to his sons: "Shem! Ham! Japheth! Make sure those giraffes don't wander away. And keep the rest of the animals in line. We need to get them all inside before the rains begin!"

Just what was going on? Why were Noah and his sons herding hundreds of animals onto a boat? It was because one day, years before, Noah had heard the word of God.

"I am very disappointed with my people," God had said to Noah. "They are wasting the lives I gave them. In all the world you are the only good man. The others do not deserve to live."

God told Noah what he was going to do: "I am going to send a great flood that will destroy the earth. Only you and your family will survive."

God had told Noah to build a floating houseboat, an ark. "Make it 450 feet long, 75 feet wide, and 45 feet high. Seal it with tar inside and out so it will be waterproof. Make sure it has three decks—bottom, middle, and upper. Put a door in the side."

Why does the ark need to be so big? Noah wondered. God told him, "You will take with you on the ark a pair of every kind of animal—male and female, wild and tame—including birds, mammals, reptiles and amphibians."

Noah had gone right to work on the ark. He did everything exactly as God had told him to do. As the ark grew bigger and bigger, people came around to watch Noah. He warned them what was going to happen, but the people just laughed. "You must be crazy," they said to Noah. But Noah didn't pay any attention to them. He went on building the ark until his hair grew white. Now, at last, it was finished.

When all the animals were on the ark, God told Noah to gather enough food and water for the animals and for his family, too, so that they could survive on the boat for a long time.

Finally, it was time for Noah, his wife, his sons, and their wives to get on the ark. Then God shut the door.

The rains began. Water came from everywhere! Not only did it fall from the sky, it also gushed out of springs and wells from underground. Rivers, streams, and lakes overflowed their banks. And the rain fell harder and harder. The people on the earth were terrified, but there was no escape.

For forty days and forty nights, the rain fell. The water on the earth got deeper and deeper, higher and higher. The water was so deep that it covered even the highest mountains, standing more than twenty-five feet above the highest peak. Only the boat with Noah, his family, and the pairs of living creatures continued to float safely on all the water. All other living things, people and animals alike, were drowned.

The water covered the entire earth for 150 days. But God had not forgotten about Noah and the animals. The terrible rains ended, and God sent a strong wind to blow across the water. He closed the places where the water had been gushing from under the ground. Slowly, the floodwaters began to recede.

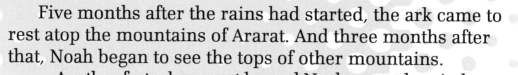

Five months after the rains had started, the ark came to rest atop the mountains of Ararat. And three months after that, Noah began to see the tops of other mountains.

Another forty days went by, and Noah opened a window and sent out a raven. The raven flew back and forth because there was no dry place to land. Next, Noah sent out a dove to see if it could find dry land. But the water was still too high, and the dove returned to the ark.

A week later, Noah tried again. He sent out the dove, and this time it came back with a green leaf from an olive tree.

"At last!" Noah said to his wife. "This means there are trees somewhere."

Noah waited for another week to pass before he released the dove again. This time it did not come back. "That means it found dry land," said Noah.

Another two months went by, and at last the earth was completely dry.

God told Noah, "Now you and your family can leave the ark. Release the animals, too, so that all of you can bring life back to the earth."

Noah and his family were grateful to God for protecting them during the flood. Noah immediately built an altar to worship God, and God was very pleased. God was so pleased that he decided he would never again destroy the earth, even though he knew people would still do evil things.

"As long as the earth remains, there will be springtime and harvest, cold and heat, winter and summer, day and night," God said.

And God sent a reminder of his promise to Noah and to all the women, men, and children who would live in later times, that he would never again send a flood to destroy the earth. God put his rainbow in the sky.

And God blessed Noah and his family.

Think about it...

People laughed at Noah when he was working on the ark, but that didn't stop him. What does that tell you about him?

All About Noah and the Flood

There are more than 500 versions of the Noah story!

They come from all over the world and date back to ancient times. Most of the stories have different details but tell of a flood that destroyed the earth. The tales from ancient Babylon and the Masai of East Africa are among the most similar to the Bible version:

1) God warns the people that a flood is coming.
2) A large floating craft is built.
3) God spares a good man, his family, and animals.

An ark is a kind of boat that floats but has no sails or engine to make it move across the water. Noah's ark was huge: nearly the length of two 747 airplanes nose to tail, and as high as a four-story building.

So where's the ark now?

When the water went down, Noah's boat came to rest on the Ararat Mountains. Although there is a Mount Ararat in modern-day Turkey, no one is certain if this is the exact mountain mentioned in the Bible. Searches still go on today in the Mount Ararat area to find the ark. In 1959, a Turkish pilot flew over the Ararat region and took photos. One of them showed a boat-shaped formation in the mountains about 500 feet long! Could it be the remains of Noah's ark? Some think maybe so, others think maybe not.

That's a lot of rain!

The flood waters were so high that the highest mountains were under almost 25 feet of water. That would mean there was 16,879 feet of water covering the earth! Compare that to the greatest amount of rain that has been recorded falling in one month—about 30 feet, in Cherrapunji, India—and the greatest amount of rain falling in one year—about 87 feet, also in Cherrapunji, India. These don't come close to the amount of rain that fell during Noah's flood, but whenever a great amount of rain causes massive flooding, we call it a flood of "biblical proportions."

DID YOU KNOW?

A picture of a dove holding an olive branch in its beak is a symbol of peace.

Never Again

Following the flood, God made a covenant, or sacred agreement, with Noah that applied to all humankind. In this covenant, God:

1. blessed and commanded Noah and his sons that they should be fruitful and multiply, and populate the earth;
2. placed all animals and plants under human command;
3. did not allow murder;
4. set up a system of justice so that violent persons will be punished;
5. promised that he will never again destroy all life on earth by flood;
6. created a rainbow as the sign of this covenant for all ages to come.

The Story of Abraham

Genesis 12–13; 15.1-6; 17; 18.1-15; 21.1-8

Long ago, God sent a flood that killed everyone on earth except Noah and his sons. As time went on, Noah's sons had sons and daughters, and their sons and daughters had children, and on and on. Now the earth was again filled with people. Many of them did not know or care about God. But God had a great plan for them, and he chose someone to help him.

God looked down upon Haran, a city of tents. The tents were homes of a group of nomads, people who spent their lives traveling from place to place.

It was here that a man named Abram lived. Abram was a simple man—not a king or a wise man, but one who faithfully worshiped the one eternal God. God knew he could trust this good man to carry out the plan he was about to put in place.

Abram was sound asleep in his tent. He woke with a start. Someone was speaking to him.

"Abram," the voice said, "I am God All-Powerful. Hear me, and do as I say. Leave this country, your people, and your father's household, and go to a land that I will show you. I will bless you, and you will be father to a great nation."

Abram was frightened. Why would God be speaking to him? And why did he, Abram, have to leave Haran, his home? But Abram didn't ask these questions.

The next day, Abram took down his tent and left the city. His wife, Sarai; his nephew, Lot; Lot's family; and all their cattle, sheep, goats, and other belongings, went with him.

They walked for many days. "How will we know this place that God has chosen for us?" Sarai asked.

"God will show us the way," Abram replied.

Their journey went on for many years and many hundreds of miles—through the desert, into the country of Egypt, and back again. When they got to the land of Canaan, Abram stopped at a place called Shechem. As he stood by a tree, he once again heard the voice of God.

"Look around you, Abram," said the voice. "This is the land that I told you about. It will belong to you and your family forever."

Abram looked in awe at the beautiful land with its rich pastures and cool streams. He built an altar to God at that very place, and thanked God for his gifts.

And God was pleased with him.

But there was still a problem. Many other nomads were camping in the same area. There wasn't enough pastureland to support all of their animals. Fights broke out between the families of Abram and Lot.

"My goats are nothing but skin over bones," said Lot. "You must give my family more land!"

"And then what are my people to do?" asked Abram. "There are three sheep feeding on every blade of grass! No, you have your fair share of what God gave to us."

Lot scowled. But then Abram had an idea.

"There's plenty of land in Canaan. Let's separate. If you go north, I'll go south. If you go south, I'll go north. Which do you want?"

Lot decided not to stay in Canaan. He saw that there was plenty of water to the east, in the valley of the Jordan River. So that's where he went.

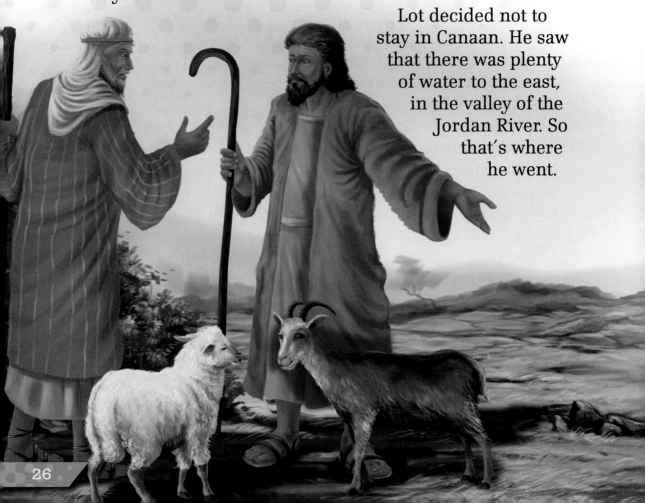

Abram Becomes Abraham

Everything was going well for Abram and his family.

He had hundreds of sheep, cattle, and goats; he had more gold and silver than he could spend. But he didn't have what he and Sarai wanted most.

One night, he went outside and prayed to God:

"Oh Lord All-Powerful, you have given me everything I could ask for. But Sarai and I are old, and we have no children. How am I to be father to a great nation? And to whom will I pass on all the gifts you have given me?"

God heard his prayer and said, "I promise that you will be the father of many nations. That's why I am now changing your name to Abraham, which means 'father of many.' And your wife's name will now be Sarah, 'mother of Israel's rulers.' You will have a son and everything you have will be his. Look up at the night sky and try to count the stars. That is the number of your children's children and those that follow them."

Abraham didn't understand how such a thing could happen, but, once again, he believed what God told him.

Three Visitors

One hot summer afternoon, Abraham was sitting at the entrance to his tent when he looked up to see three men standing nearby. They looked tired, as if they had been on the road for days. Abraham got up quickly and went to greet them.

"My friends, please, come to my home and rest," he said. "I'll have some water brought so that you can wash your dusty feet. You can rest under the trees while my wife prepares some food for you."

"That's very kind of you," the men said.

Abraham went into his tent and asked Sarah to make some fresh bread. He asked his servant to roast some meat. When everything was ready, Abraham took the meat and a jug of milk out to his guests. He stood under some trees while they ate.

When they had finished, one of the guests said to Abraham, "You are a good man, Abraham. Where is Sarah, your wife?"

"She is in the tent," Abraham answered.

"Tell her that she no longer has to weep for the child she never had. I'll return about this time next year. When I do, you and Sarah will already have a son."

Abraham was amazed. How did this stranger know what he and Sarah had always longed for? But at that moment, Abraham looked into the man's eyes. Suddenly he knew that this was not a man at all. It was God himself. Somehow, though, Abraham didn't feel afraid.

Inside the tent, Sarah had been listening. She couldn't believe her ears. How could she have a child now, when other women her age were grandmothers many times over? She couldn't help but laugh.

God heard her. "Why is Sarah laughing?" he asked. "I am the Lord your God. Nothing is too difficult for me!"

Sarah stopped laughing and began to believe with all her heart.

God was good to Sarah and kept his promise. Within a year, she and Abraham had a son. They named their baby Isaac, which means 'laughter.' He was the joy of their old age, and a sign that all of God's promises would come true.

Think about it...

God showed his love for Abraham in many ways. In what ways has God shown his love for you?

All About Abraham

There are people today who choose to be nomads, often moving from one place to another. They may live in tents, or have a home on wheels, such as a motor home, a camper, or a type of wagon called a caravan.

You're Welcome!

In Bible times, many people lived in the desert. When people came to your home, you had to welcome them in, even if you didn't know them. It was the rule, and sometimes a matter of life and death! If they were your enemies, you still had to treat them as guests and offer them water, food, and shelter. You had to make sure your guests' animals had water and food, too. So when three strangers came to Abraham's tent, Abraham immediately offered them a place to sit in the shade, water to wash their feet, and some carefully prepared food.

Home Sweet Home

While we enjoy sleeping in tents on a camping trip, can you imagine living in one as your home? Tents in Bible times, however, were the only homes nomads like Abraham's family had. Tents were made of goat and camel hair that was woven together into a thick, heavy cloth. When this cloth got wet, the animal hair would shrink, making it nearly waterproof. Men and women lived in separate tents. A group of tents would be set up in a circle, with the leader's tent in the middle. He would stick his spear in the ground to show that he was in charge.

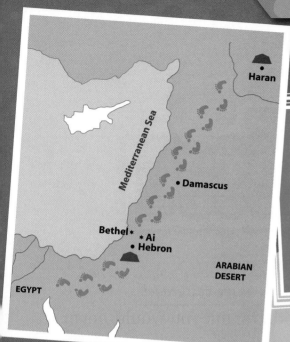

A Long, Long Walk

It is safe to say that Abraham traveled more than 1,000 miles after leaving Haran until he finally settled in Hebron. This includes the trip to and from Egypt, but not the time he spent wandering in the desert.

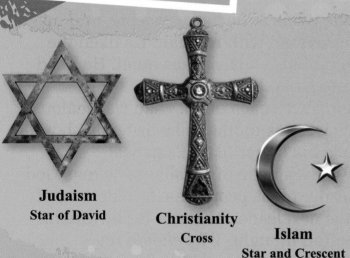

Judaism
Star of David

Christianity
Cross

Islam
Star and Crescent

DID YOU KNOW?

Jews, Muslims, and Christians all claim Abraham as the "father" of their religion. That's more than 3 billion people!

Abraham to the Rescue

After Abraham had settled in Canaan, a war broke out in the land where his nephew, Lot, was living. Lot was captured and taken to a city far away in the north. When Abraham found out, he formed an army of 318 men and led them into the fight. They defeated the enemy who had captured his nephew, and brought Lot back home with him as well as all the others that had been taken.

Genesis 25; 27

Abraham's son, Isaac, became the second leader of God's people. He had two sons, Jacob and Esau. One of them would be the next leader.

Jacob and Esau were twin brothers, but you would never know it.

Esau, the first of the twins to be born, was big, and his arms and hands were covered with red hair. He liked the outdoors and was a good hunter. Jacob was quiet. He liked living out in a tent among his flock of sheep.

They didn't get along with each other. Esau was jealous of Jacob because Jacob was his mother's favorite; Jacob was jealous of Esau because his father liked Esau best.

Now, their father was Isaac, son of Abraham, the man God had chosen to be the leader of his people. As the older son of Isaac, Esau would be the next leader. This was his birthright.

It isn't fair, Jacob often thought. *Why should my brother be the next leader just because he's a few minutes older than I?*

One day, Jacob was cooking some bean stew when Esau came up to his tent. Esau had been hunting all day. "Give me some of that stew," he growled. "I'm starving."

Jacob was very sly, and he saw a chance to get what he felt should be his.

"Sell me your birthright as the first born son," he said, "and I'll give you some food."

Esau didn't take time to think about it. "I'm about to die of hunger. What good would my birthright do me now?"

"So," said Jacob, "you promise to sell me your birthright here and now?"

"I said so, didn't I?" Esau replied. "Now give me some food!"

Jacob smiled as he gave his brother a bowl of bean stew and some bread. Now he, not Esau, would be the next leader of their people.

After Esau finished eating, he got up and left. That's how little he cared about his birthright.

The Hands of Esau

In time, Isaac grew very old and became blind. He wanted to give Esau the blessing that would make him the leader.

He called his favorite son to his bedside.

"I may die at any time," he told Esau. "Go out with your bow and arrows and kill a wild animal. Then cook it the way I like so much and bring it to me. I want to taste it one last time and give you my blessing."

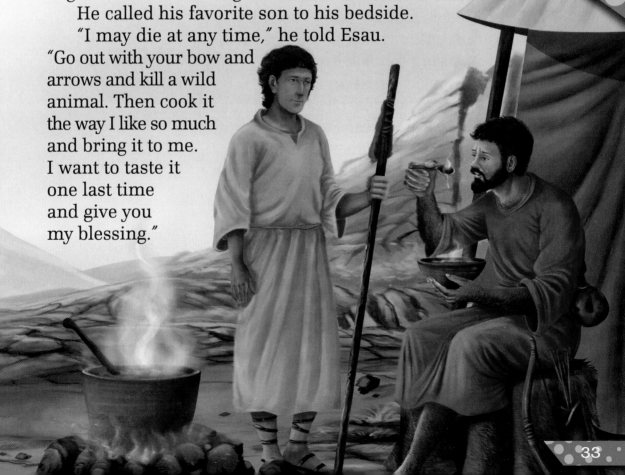

33

Isaac's wife, Rebekah, had heard everything. "Oh, no," she said to herself. "This cannot happen." She knew something that her husband did not. Before the twins were born, God had spoken to her and told her that the younger twin would be the next leader of the people. Somehow, she would have to make Isaac give his blessing to Jacob.

The minute Esau left, she ran to Jacob. She told him what was happening.

"Hurry, my son. This is what you must do: Go and kill two of your best goats and bring them to me. I will cook them the way your father likes. Then you can take it to him and he will give you his blessing before he dies."

Jacob saw a problem with this plan. "My brother is a hairy man," he said. "What if my father touches me? He will know I'm trying to trick him."

Rebekah said, "Just do as I say."

A short time later, Jacob sat at his father's bedside. He was wearing Esau's best clothes and his arms and hands were covered with hairy skins that Rebekah had taken from the goats.

"Who is there?" Isaac asked.

"Father, it is I, Esau," Jacob said, trying to make his voice sound like his brother's. "I have brought you the meal you asked for."

Then Isaac said, "Your voice sounds strange. Come closer to me. I want to touch you to see if you really are Esau."

Jacob bent down so Isaac could touch him and smell him. Isaac said, "You sound like Jacob, but your hands feel hairy, like Esau's, and your clothes smell of him."

And then Isaac blessed Jacob, thinking he was Esau.

A little while later, Esau went into Isaac's tent. "Father, here is the meat you asked me to bring. Eat it and then give me your blessing."

"Who are you?" Isaac asked.

"It is I, Esau, your first-born son," Esau told him.

Isaac was startled. "Then it must have been Jacob who was here before. He tricked me and stole your blessing!"

Esau cursed Jacob. Then he started to cry. "Can't you give me a blessing, too?" he begged his father.

Isaac was as upset as Esau. "I cannot take back the blessing I gave to Jacob. I can only make this promise to you: You will make your home far away where it is good for farming. You will live by the power of your sword and be your brother's slave. But when you decide to be free, you will break loose."

Rebekah could see how angry Esau was. She said to Jacob, "You will have to run away from here or your brother will kill you. Go to my brother Laban's house in the city of Haran. When Esau stops being angry, I'll send for you to come home."

It was many years before Esau forgave his brother. Jacob stayed in Haran, got married, and had children. When at last he returned home, Rebekah was not there to greet him. She had died without ever seeing her favorite son again.

Think about it...

Who do you think really deserved the birthright? Why do you think so?

All About Jacob and Esau

What's in a Name?

The names of Rebekah and Isaac's twins told a lot about each son. When Esau was born, he was covered with red hair. His name, "Esau," was a play on the Hebrew word for "hairy." Jacob's name means "he takes by the heel," because he was born grabbing on to his older brother's foot.

DID YOU KNOW?

Twins of different sexes or who don't look alike are called fraternal twins. (Fraternal means brotherly, but the term is used for girls, too.) Twins who look alike are called identical twins.

GOD AND JACOB

After Jacob left home, he had a dream. He saw a ladder going from earth to heaven with God's angels going up and down the steps. God was standing next to him and told him that he would give Jacob and his family the land that he had promised to Abraham and Isaac, and Jacob would have a huge number of descendents who would live all over the earth.

Later, God came to Jacob again and gave him the name, "Israel." Jacob's twelve sons would become the leaders of twelve tribes in the new nation of Israel. Their names were Reuben, Simeon, Levi, Judah, Issachar, Zebulon, Gad, Asher, Dan, Naphtali, Joseph, and Benjamin.

Joseph, the Dreamer

Genesis 37; 39–41

Jacob's large family lived in the land of Canaan, where his father Isaac had lived. This is the story of his family.

Jacob wanted to give something special to his favorite son, Joseph. He made a beautiful coat with stripes of different colors.

"Thank you, father," Joseph said as he put the coat on. "I can't wait to show it to my brothers."

That was the trouble with Joseph. He was always bragging and showing off, and his ten older brothers couldn't stand him. Only the youngest, Benjamin, liked him. So when Joseph showed off his coat, his brothers only grumbled.

Then Joseph made things even worse.

A few days after Jacob gave him the coat, Joseph had a dream. In the dream, he and his older brothers were out in the field, tying long strands of wheat into bundles. His bundle stood up. Then all the other bundles stood up around it and bowed to it.

Naturally, Joseph wasted no time in telling his brothers about it.

They laughed.

"What do we care about a dream?" said Simeon. "We aren't bundles of wheat, and we will never bow down to you."

But Joseph soon had another dream. This time, he told his father. In the dream, the sun and moon and eleven stars were all bowing down to him. Even Jacob thought he had gone too far this time. "What's that supposed to mean?" he said. "Are your Mother and I and your brothers all going to come and bow down in front of you?"

Angry, he sent the boy away. But secretly, he wondered if there really could be something to Joseph's visions.

Twenty Pieces of Silver

One morning, Jacob sent Joseph to check up on his brothers who were out in a pasture tending sheep. Joseph put on his coat of many colors and set off.

Two hours later, the brothers saw him coming across the field.

"Look! Here comes the great dreamer," Dan said. The sight of Joseph in his fancy coat made the brothers' blood boil.

"Here's a chance for us to get rid of that pest," Simeon said.

"Let's kill him and bury him out here. We can tell our father that some wild animals did it."

Most of the brothers agreed. But Reuben, the oldest, didn't want harm to come to Joseph.

"We don't have to kill him," he said. "Let's throw him in this pit and let him die." Secretly, Reuben was planning to go back later and rescue Joseph.

When Joseph got near, the brothers grabbed him and tore off his coat.

"Stop!" Joseph cried. "What are you doing?"

His brothers lifted him up and threw him in the pit.

The pit was deep and Joseph could not climb out. "What good are your dreams now?" Simeon said, and the brothers sat down to eat.

Soon, some traders came by on their way to Egypt, their camels loaded with spices and perfumes to sell.

By this time, the brothers had cooled down a little.

Judah said, "I have an idea. Instead of killing Joseph, why don't we sell him as a slave to the traders? After all, he is our brother."

They all thought this was a good plan, and they sold Joseph to the merchants for twenty pieces of silver.

"What are we going to tell our father?" Dan asked.

The brothers talked it over for a while. Then they killed a goat and dipped Joseph's coat in the blood. They took the coat to Jacob.

"We found this out in the field," Judah told him, forcing tears from his eyes.

Jacob knew right away it was Joseph's coat. He fell to his knees and pulled at his hair, crying, "Oh my poor son, eaten by wild animals! I will never see him again."

The brothers never said a word. None of them knew that God had something special in mind for Joseph.

Joseph in Prison

Far away in Egypt, Joseph was alive and well. The traders had sold him to a rich man named Potiphar who worked at the palace of Pharaoh, the ruler of Egypt.

Potiphar took a liking to Joseph. He could tell that Joseph was smart and able to handle important work, so he put Joseph in charge of his house and all his property.

Everything was going well until the wife of Potiphar noticed how handsome and strong Joseph was. She began to flirt with him.

Joseph tried to stay away from her. He didn't want to anger Potiphar. But the wife kept after him. Finally, he told her to stay far away from him. He turned to leave, but she grabbed at his coat. A piece ripped off in her hand as Joseph hurried away.

The wife was angry that Joseph had rejected her. She went to her husband and showed him the piece of Joseph's coat.

"That Joseph tried to attack me," she said. "But I got away. See, this piece of his coat tore off when I escaped."

Potiphar believed this lie. He ordered his men to take Joseph to Pharaoh's prison and put him with the other prisoners.

More Dreams

In the prison, Joseph met a man who had once been Pharaoh's butler. The butler had done something that made Pharaoh angry, so Pharaoh had sent him to jail.

One day, the man seemed upset.

"What's wrong?" Joseph asked.

"I had a strange dream last night," the man told him. "I wish I knew what it meant."

"Tell me about the dream," Joseph said. "God knows what

dreams mean and he will help me give you the answer."

The butler told Joseph his dream.

"I saw a vine with three branches. Grapes grew on the vine. I held Pharaoh's cup under the grapes and squeezed them. Then I gave the cup to Pharaoh."

"This is a good dream," Joseph said. "It means that in three days, Pharaoh will pardon you. You will once again be his butler."

This made the butler very happy.

Three days later, the guards came to take the butler back to the palace. Within a week, the butler had forgotten all about Joseph.

For two more years, Joseph remained in prison. But then something happened that even he would never have expected. Pharaoh himself had a dream. He was standing beside the Nile River. Suddenly, seven fat, healthy cows came up from the river and started eating the grass along the bank. Then seven ugly, skinny cows came up out of the river and ate the fat, healthy cows.

What could the dream mean? Pharaoh asked his wise men. But none of them knew the answer. Then the butler remembered Joseph.

"Tell my guards to bring this man to me," Pharaoh said.

In a short time, Joseph stood before Pharaoh and Pharaoh told him the dream.

Joseph replied, "O great king, this is what your dream means: The seven fat cows stand for seven years of good weather when there will be plenty of grain. The seven skinny cows stand for seven years of bad weather so that grain won't grow and there will be a great famine. People will starve."

Then he went on:

"God has told me the meaning of this dream so that you can save your people. In the years of plenty, you should set aside one-fifth of the wheat crop and store it away. Then, when the bad years come, there will be enough wheat to get by."

Pharaoh liked the plan. Not only that. He liked Joseph. *This is no ordinary slave,* he thought. *This is an exceptional man, someone I can trust.*

He put Joseph in charge of the palace. Joseph did such a good job that Pharaoh gave him a promotion. He made Joseph governor of the land. He gave him a chariot of his own so he could check up on all the various parts of the country.

Now he was the second most powerful man in all of Egypt, but he hadn't forgotten his family back in Canaan. Was his father still alive? And his brothers—were they sorry for what they had done to him?

It would not be long before he found out.

Think about it...

Joseph had to go through some terrible times. What do you think gives people the strength to survive hard times in their lives?

All About Joseph, the Dreamer

The Power of Pharaoh

Pharaoh is the name the Egyptian people gave to their king. He was the most important person in Egypt. The people believed he was a god-king and it was up to him to make sure that all the laws set down by the Egyptian gods were followed. If the Pharaoh failed to do this, the Egyptians believed that the whole world would fall apart!

What was really so special about Joseph's Coat?

Most coats in those days were sleeveless, like long open vests. Usually, only wealthy men had coats with long sleeves.

Dream On

- Everybody dreams, but no one knows for sure why.
- Most people forget their dreams within ten minutes of waking up.
- You can tell when someone is dreaming when you see their eyelids twitch. Sometimes, you may see this happen to your cat or dog. Do you wonder what they are dreaming about?

Funny Money

The pieces of silver the brothers got when they sold Joseph were called shekels. Today, the word is used as a slang for "money." In fact, the currency now used in the state of Israel is called the Israeli new shekel.

JOSEPH ON STAGE

The story of Joseph is one of the best-loved stories in the Bible. It's even been made into a musical! *Joseph and the Amazing Technicolor Dreamcoat* by Sir Andrew Lloyd Webber and Tim Rice has been playing all over the world since 1967.

DID YOU KNOW?

Chariots were the earliest kind of two-wheeled, horse-drawn vehicles. In Egypt, chariots began to be used in 1500 B.C., after the first horses were brought into the country.

Joseph in Egypt

Genesis 41.53–57; 42–46

The story of Joseph and his brothers continues.

Joseph had been right about the meaning of Pharaoh's dream. The next seven years were the fat cows: wheat and barley sprung like magic from the land. The storage rooms soon were filled with grain. More storage rooms were built. Then came the skinny cows: the hot, dry weather. Water became scarce and plants withered and died.

The seven years of famine had begun.

It was time to open the storehouses. Every day people came from all over Egypt, and from other countries as well, to buy the grain that would keep them from starving. They had to come before Joseph who was in charge of selling the grain.

One day, ten men walked into the storeroom. Joseph knew right away who they were—his brothers! The brothers didn't know that this handsome man, wearing fine clothes and a gold chain, was the boy they had sold as a slave so many years before.

What should he do? Joseph wanted to forgive them, but he needed to know if they felt sorry for what they had done to him. He decided to test them.

"Where are you from?" he asked in a rude voice.

"We come from the land of Canaan," Reuben said, "to buy grain."

"I don't believe you!" Joseph snapped. "You're all spies, come to Egypt to find out where our country is weak so that you can attack us."

"No, no!" the brothers said. "We're honest men."

Reuben spoke up. "We're all from the same family. We have wives and children and a father and younger brother back in Canaan. They are waiting for us to bring grain because we are starving."

When he heard them mention his father and brother, Joseph almost wept. His heart ached to see them.

He had an idea.

"Well," he said, "if you are honest men, you will do as I order. One of you must stay here, and the others can take the grain back to your families. You must bring your youngest brother to me. Then I'll know you're telling the truth. If you don't return with him, I will kill the man you leave here."

So Simeon was tied up and taken away. The nine others started on their way back to Canaan.

The Brothers Return

When Jacob heard the story, he shook his head.

"No, I won't let you take Benjamin to Egypt. What if something happens to him? I've already lost one son, and I'll die from sorrow if I lose my youngest one."

"But," said Judah, "if we don't bring Benjamin to the governor, he will kill Simeon. Let Benjamin go with me. I promise to bring him back safely."

Finally, Jacob gave in. "You may all go, but take some gifts along. Perhaps then the governor will treat you more kindly. I pray that God All-Powerful will be good to you and that the governor will let Simeon and Benjamin come back home with you."

When the brothers reached Joseph's house, they were quickly brought inside.

"Here is our brother, Benjamin," Judah told Joseph.

Joseph was so happy to see his young brother that he

wanted to celebrate, but he tried hard not to show it. He told his guards to let Simeon out of jail.

"You have proven your honesty," Joseph said to his brothers. "Please be my guests at dinner tonight."

Joseph put his brothers at a table in front of his own table. They were amazed to see that they were seated in order of their ages, the oldest to the youngest. How did the governor know? They were served food from Joseph's table, and Benjamin was given five times as much as the others.

The Silver Cup

Joseph was ready to move on to the last part of his plan. He told his servants, "Fill the men's grain sacks and put my silver cup in the sack of the youngest brother."

The brothers left the next morning with the sacks of grain tied onto their donkeys.

They had not gone far when one of Joseph's men came riding up in a chariot. He accused them of stealing the cup.

"We haven't stolen anything. We are not thieves!" Reuben said. "Look in our sacks. If you find that one of us has the cup, then kill him. The rest of us will become your slaves."

The man opened the sacks one at a time, leaving Benjamin's for last. When he pulled out the silver cup, the brothers were overcome with sorrow. Why was this happening to them? Could it be that God was punishing them for what they did to their brother, Joseph, all those years ago?

Sadly they turned around and headed back to the governor's house.

A Joyful Reunion

Joseph looked at his brothers bowing down to him. This is just what he had dreamed when he was a boy.

Judah said, "Sir, we don't know how this happened. How can we say we are innocent? God has shown us we are guilty, and now we are your slaves."

Joseph said, "I would never punish all of you. Only the one who had the cup will stay here as my slave. The rest of you are free to go home to your father."

Judah put his hand on Benjamin's shoulder. "Please, no," he said. "Our father loves Benjamin so much that he will die of sorrow if we don't bring him back with us. Let me stay and be your slave, instead."

Joseph could no longer pretend. He knew now that his

brothers had changed and had become good men. He sent his servants out of the room and turned to his family.

"I am your brother, Joseph," he said, his eyes filled with tears. "The one you sold and sent to Egypt."

Now his brothers were really afraid, but Joseph comforted them.

"Don't worry or blame yourselves for what you did. God is the one who sent me ahead of you to save lives."

Joseph told his brothers to go back to Canaan and bring their father and all their families and animals to Egypt.

Then he waited. The days and weeks went by and every day Joseph prayed and thanked God for his good fortune. And now, his whole family would be together!

One morning, he heard the sound of many voices in the distance. A crowd of seventy people was coming toward him. His family!

He ran to greet them.

The first person he saw was the one he had missed most of all—Jacob, his father.

He hugged him around his neck and cried for a long time. Jacob was crying, too.

"Oh my son," he said. "Now that I have seen you, there is nothing more I will want for the rest of my life."

And so, Jacob's family came to live in Egypt, in the land of Goshen.

Think about it...

In spite of all the terrible things that happened to him, why was Joseph able to forgive his brothers? And why didn't Joseph feel angry with God? Do you think God guides your life in the same way?

All About Joseph in Egypt

Table manners

Joseph ate by himself because Egyptians considered themselves better than other people, especially shepherds and nomads. As a Hebrew, Joseph could not eat with the other Egyptians—even though he outranked them! As foreigners and shepherds, Joseph's brothers were even lower in rank, so they had to eat at a separate table, too.

A LIFE IN EGYPT

When Joseph began a new life in Egypt, he was given the name Zaphenath-Paneah, which means "revealer of secrets." He married an Egyptian woman and had two sons. He lived there until he died.

DID YOU KNOW?

The famous pyramids of Giza in Egypt were built more than 1,000 years before Joseph's time.

The Silver Cup

Joseph's silver cup was a symbol of his authority. It was thought to have supernatural powers, so to steal it was a serious crime. Such cups were used for predicting the future. A person poured water into the cup and saw images in the reflections, ripples, and bubbles. Joseph really didn't need this silver cup, since God told him everything he needed to know about the future.

Joseph's Bones

When Joseph died, he was buried in Egypt. He made his children promise that one day, when they returned to the Promised Land, they would take his bones with them. That didn't happen until Moses led the Israelites out of Egypt 400 years later! Joseph's bones were finally buried by his descendants in the town of Shechem.

Bread of Life

Bread made from the available grain, mostly wheat and barley, was one of the most important foods of the ancient Near East. Bread was so basic a food that the same word was used for both. "Breaking bread" meant the same as "having a meal." The best breads were made from wheat flour. Barley, a hardier grain that could grow on poorer soil, was used to feed animals. During a famine, barley was the last source of nourishment to be found.

The Story of Moses

Exodus 1–4

The story of Moses is one of the most exciting stories in the Bible. It begins when Moses was just a baby.

A woman named Jochabed and her young daughter, Miriam, stood at the banks of the Nile River in Egypt. In her arms, the woman held a basket. Inside the basket was something precious to her—her baby son.

Slowly, the woman walked into the water. She set the basket down where the tall grass grew and came back to shore.

The basket floated on the water.

"Miriam," the woman said. "Stay here and keep an eye on him. Tell me what happens." The woman took one last look at the basket and walked away. She prayed to the God of Israel to look after her son and spare him from the terrible fate of other Hebrew baby boys.

Hebrews had been living in Egypt since the time of Jacob and Joseph. Now there were many thousands—so many that Pharaoh, the king, was afraid they would take over the whole country. So he forced the Hebrews into doing hard labor, working in the fields and making bricks to build new cities. They lived like slaves. But still, their numbers grew.

Finally, Pharaoh thought of a way to solve the problem.

He sent out a horrible order to all the people of Egypt: all newborn Hebrew baby boys were to be thrown into the Nile to drown; the girls could live.

Jochabed had been hiding her baby for three months. She knew she couldn't keep him hidden much longer. When she put him in the river, she prayed that someone would find him and give him a safe home.

God heard her prayer.

Just after Jochabed left, one of Pharaoh's daughters came down to take a bath in the river. The princess saw the basket in the tall grass.

"Go and fetch that basket," she said to her servants. "I want to see what's inside."

The servants were smiling when they brought her the basket.

"A baby!" the princess cried. She knew at once that it must be a Hebrew child.

"Poor little boy," she said. "You don't deserve to die. I will keep you with me, and you will be safe."

From a distance, Miriam had seen and heard everything. She approached the princess and bowed down to her.

"Great lady," she said, "you are kind to rescue this child. You will need someone to nurse him. I know a Hebrew woman who would be glad to help you."

The princess smiled. "Go and bring this woman to me," she said.

Miriam ran home, and in a short time she came back to the palace with the woman—it was her mother, Jochabed.

The princess handed her the baby.

"Take good care of him. I will pay you. When he is weaned, bring him back to me."

And so it was that Jochabed was able to keep her son for three more years. Then she took him back to the palace.

The princess adopted him and gave him the name, Moses.

Moses grew into a handsome, strong young man. As a prince, he had a good life. He had only the best clothing, food and drink. He had servants to take care of all his needs, so he had plenty of time for fun.

One day, the princess told him the secret she had kept from him all this time. "Moses, I have loved you like a son, but I am not your real mother. I found you in a basket in the Nile River. You belong to the Hebrew people."

A Hebrew! Moses was stunned. He wouldn't believe it!

He then learned that Jochabed was his real mother, and that he had an older sister and brother, Miriam and Aaron. They were good people, and he soon came to love them.

As time went on, Moses saw how badly his people were being treated. He saw the slave overseers whip any Hebrew worker, man or woman, who had stopped to rest. The more he saw, the angrier he became. One day, he got so angry that he attacked an overseer who was beating a worker.

Before he knew it, the Egyptian was dead. He buried the man in the sand.

Pharaoh heard about what Moses had done and said, "He cannot get away with murder! Moses must die!"

The next day, Moses left the city. Pharaoh sent his men after him, but Moses escaped.

A New Life

For days and days, Moses walked across deserts and over mountains. At last, he came to the land of Midian. The people there were descendents of Abraham, the father of the Israelites. Now Moses was among his own people.

One day, Moses was sitting by a well. Seven women came to water their father's sheep and goats. Just then, some shepherds arrived and tried to chase the women away.

"Get out of here!" Moses yelled at the shepherds. They ran off, and Moses watered the women's animals.

The women told their father, Jethro, about the man who had rescued them at the well.

"Where is he?" Jethro asked. "Why did you leave him there? Invite him to eat with us."

When Moses arrived, Jethro welcomed him. In no time, the two men were like father and son. Moses stayed and married one of Jethro's daughters. He became a shepherd, like his father-in-law.

God Chooses Moses

One day, Moses was taking care of Jethro's sheep and goats. He decided to take them through the desert to a mountain called Sinai.

Moses walked all morning and into the afternoon. Suddenly, he stopped. There, in front of him, was a bush on fire! But the fire wasn't burning up the bush.

That's very strange, Moses thought. He went closer to get a better look at the bush.

Then someone called out his name, "Moses!" The voice seemed to be coming from inside the flames!

"Don't come any closer," the voice said. "Take off your sandals. You are standing on holy ground. I am the God who was worshiped by your ancestors Abraham, Isaac, and Jacob."

Moses was afraid to look at God, so he hid his face.

God said, "I have seen how my people are suffering in Egypt. I have heard them beg for help. So I will take them out of Egypt to a country where there is good land, rich with milk and honey.

"Now, go to Pharaoh! I have chosen you to lead my people out of his country."

Moses was alarmed. "Why me?" he asked. "I am a simple shepherd, not a leader."

"I will be with you," God told him. "And you will worship me on this mountain after you take my people out of Egypt."

These words gave Moses courage.

"I will tell the people of Israel that you have sent me," he said. "But what should I say if they ask me your name?"

God said to Moses, "I am the eternal God, so tell them that the Lord, whose name is 'I Am', has sent you."

Moses was still worried. He asked God, "What if no one believes that you really appeared to me?"

God answered, "You have a walking stick in your hand. Throw it down!"

Moses threw the stick onto the ground. At once, it turned into a snake! Moses jumped back.

"Pick it up by the tail," God told him. When Moses did this, the snake turned back into a walking stick.

"If no one believes this miracle," God said, "take some water from the Nile and pour it on the ground. It will turn to blood."

Still, Moses had some doubt. "I am not a good speaker," he said to God. "I am slow at speaking, and can never think of what to say."

God replied, "Who makes people able to speak or makes them deaf or unable to speak? Don't you know I am the one who does this?"

Moses begged, "Lord, please choose someone else."

God was not pleased with Moses, but he said, "Your brother, Aaron, is on his way to see you. He is a good speaker. You will tell him what to say.

"Now, leave the land of Midian and return to Egypt. Everyone who wanted to kill you is dead."

When Moses returned home, he went to see his father-in-law. He did not tell Jethro what had happened, but instead he said, "I have been thinking of my people in Egypt. I would like to go back there and see if any of them are still alive."

"If that is what you want, you should go," Jethro said.

The next day, Moses put his wife and sons on a donkey and started on the road that would take them to Egypt.

In his hand, he carried the walking stick he had used to show God's power.

Think about it...

Moses wasn't sure he could do what God had asked him. Have you been asked to do something you felt you couldn't do? What did you do?

All About Moses

Famous First

Miriam, Moses' older sister, was the first woman in the Bible to be called a prophet.

Basket Making

An Egyptian basket turned out to be a good boat for baby Moses. Because wood was scarce in ancient Egypt, the Egyptians rarely made wooden boxes. Instead, they wove sturdy baskets from various grasses, twigs, and leaves. They also wove sandals, mats, and blankets.

NAMING THE BABY

In Egyptian, Moses means "one who draws." So it was a perfect name for a baby who was drawn out (or pulled out) of the water. The ancient Hebrews pronounced the name, "Moshe" (mo-SHEH).

Oops!

This famous statue by Michelangelo shows two horns coming out of Moses' head. Why would the sculptor give Moses horns? Some Bible experts think it was because of a mistake made by Saint Jerome when he was translating the Bible from Hebrew into Latin. Saint Jerome may have been confused by the Hebrew word *keren*, which can mean either "radiated light" [was shining] or "grew horns." The first meaning is the correct translation of the Bible passage [Exodus 34. 29—35], but for years people believed that Moses had grown horns when he came down from Mount Sinai with the Ten Commandments.

Where is the land of milk and honey?

You won't find the name on any road map, but the "land of milk and honey" was located in what today is the land of Israel. Today, people use the phrase to describe a place where there is plenty of everything that people need.

No Sandals Allowed

The ancient Hebrews took off their sandals and shoes when entering a temple, home, or sacred land. They also took off their sandals when mourning the death of a loved one. At the time, travelers often carried the sandals slung over their shoulders during a long journey. When they arrived in a new town, they would wash their feet and put on their sandals again.

DID YOU KNOW?

A burning bush is a decorative plant with red leaves. It was named after the bush from which God spoke to Moses on Mount Sinai.

The Exodus

Exodus 5–12

Moses and Aaron go to Pharaoh with a message from God. But Pharaoh will not listen, so God punishes all the Egyptians.

After leaving Midian, Moses once more entered the Sinai Desert, leading his family toward Egypt. Every step brought him closer to his meeting with Pharaoh.

Pharaoh will only laugh when I tell him why I've come, Moses thought. *Why did God choose me for this terrible task?*

As the family neared Mount Sinai, a man came walking toward them. It was Aaron! Just as God had said, he had been on the way to visit Moses.

When they got to Egypt, Moses and Aaron knew that they must first tell the people why they had come. The brothers called a meeting of all the leaders of Israel and showed them the miracles that God could do through Moses.

Hope filled the hearts of the leaders. They gave thanks to God. "The Lord has shown us that we will soon be free," they said.

Then Moses and Aaron went to the palace and stood before Pharaoh. Aaron spoke the words that God told to Moses.

"The Lord God says, 'Let my people go into the desert, so they can honor me with a celebration there.'"

Pharaoh laughed.

"Who is this Lord and why should I obey him? No, I will not let your people go!" Then Pharaoh leaned forward. "And hear this. I am told that the Hebrews stopped working after you spoke to them. So because of you, they will now work even harder!"

Pharaoh ordered all the slave overseers to stop giving the workers the straw they needed to make bricks. The workers had to gather their own straw and still make the same number of bricks they had before. When the workers couldn't do this, the overseers called them lazy and beat them with whips until they were bleeding.

Now the leaders of Israel were angry with Aaron and Moses. "Our people suffer more now than before," they said.

Moses prayed to God for help. God answered, "You will soon see what I will do to the king. He will let my people go, and he will even chase them out of this country."

Once again, Moses and Aaron went to see Pharaoh.

Again, Aaron told him, "The Lord God says, 'Let my people go.' If you do not, God will use his powers to destroy you."

"What powers?" Pharaoh asked. "I haven't seen your God do anything."

At once, Aaron threw down the walking stick and it turned into a snake.

The people were amazed, but Pharaoh looked bored. He called for his magicians who had their own secret powers. The magicians threw down their sticks. Everyone gasped as the magicians' sticks turned into snakes, too.

But in the next second, Aaron's snake swallowed the others.

"It's still only a trick," Pharaoh said. And he would not change his mind.

God told Moses and Aaron, "This is just the beginning. I tell you the king will go on being stubborn until it is time for you to take my people to freedom. Now listen to me, and I will tell you what you must do."

For the third time, Moses and Aaron stood before Pharaoh, and Aaron delivered another message. "The Lord has sent us to punish all of Egypt. Come with us to the Nile River and we will show you what God can do."

Curious, the king and his officials followed Moses and Aaron to the banks of the Nile. Aaron plunged his walking stick into the river. At once, all the water turned to blood! Not only that, every drop of water in the country turned to blood—water in wells, in jars, in buckets. The fish in the river died and the river began to stink.

Even this wasn't enough to make the Pharaoh change his mind. Hadn't his magicians performed similar tricks in the past? But the people of Egypt and their animals were soon thirsty, and the crops began to wither. The Egyptians had to dig deep wells to get enough fresh water to live.

Seven days later, the Lord sent Moses and Aaron back to Pharaoh. God said, "Tell the king that if he does not let my people go, I will cover all of Egypt with frogs."

Just as God had known he would, Pharaoh still refused to listen. So Aaron held his stick over the Nile. At once, frogs began leaping out of the water. They came out of every river and every pond. They hopped into every room in every house. They even got into the bowls of bread dough and into the ovens.

Pharaoh sent for Moses and Aaron.

"Get rid of these frogs," he said, "and I will let your people go into the desert to worship your God."

So Moses begged the Lord to do something about the frogs. The next day, all the frogs, except those in the Nile River, died. The dead frogs were stacked into piles and the whole country began to stink.

But once the frogs were gone, Pharaoh turned stubborn again, and he did not keep his promise.

God's Powers

Moses and Aaron went to see Pharaoh seven more times. And every time he refused to let God's people go, God sent another horrible plague upon the land:

...Every speck of dust in Egypt turned into a biting, stinging gnat. The gnats swarmed on the people and animals until their skin bled.

...Buzzing flies filled the air, spreading disease.

...All the cattle, sheep, and goats belonging to Egyptians became sick and died.

...Painful, burning sores covered every inch of skin on all the people and animals.

...A hailstorm pounded the earth, flattening the crops and injuring any living thing that was caught outside.

...A swarm of locusts ate the leaves of every plant and every tree, so that nothing green remained in Egypt.

...The sky turned completely black, and a terrifying darkness covered Egypt for three days.

The people of Egypt suffered greatly during these times, but the people of Israel, who lived separately in the land of Goshen, were spared.

After the ninth disaster, God sent Moses to Pharaoh one last time. By now, Pharaoh had had enough.

"Go!" he said. "Take your families with you. But leave your sheep, goats, and cattle here."

"The animals must go, too. We need them to live," Moses said.

This was too much for Pharaoh. He leapt to his feet, "Then you get nothing! Leave me and don't come back!"

The Final Disaster

God had planned everything that had happened in Egypt.

Now it was time for him to punish the Egyptians in a way that would make Pharaoh beg the Israelites to leave the country.

He told Moses what he wanted the people to do, and Moses made sure they were ready.

So it happened that on the fourteenth day of the month, every family prepared a special feast in honor of the Lord. The door of every house was marked with a brush dipped in lamb's blood.

That night, they roasted the lamb and served it with bitter herbs and flat bread that was made without yeast. The Israelites had been warned to stay inside no matter what they might hear or see, for the most terrible disaster of all was about to strike the people of Egypt.

During the night, an angel of God swept through the country, taking the lives of the first-born son in every Egyptian family. But the angel passed over all the houses that had the mark of blood on the door.

Soon the cries and wails of the families who had lost a son could be heard in every house. And no one cried and mourned more than Pharaoh, whose own first-born son had been his favorite child.

That night, Pharaoh sent for Moses and Aaron. He said, "Take your people and animals out of my country now. Go and worship the Lord. But ask your God to be kind to me."

The Egyptians went to the Israelites and begged them to leave right away.

It was exactly four hundred and thirty years after the people of Israel had first arrived in Egypt. At that time, there were seventy people. Now their numbers had grown to six hundred thousand. Moses led them, plus their animals and many other people who wanted to go with them, out of Egypt to the city of Succoth.

Think about it...

The power of the Lord can be frightening, and it can also bring great joy. What are some of the ways that God has shown his powers in the world today?

All About the Exodus

Nice Neighbors

Just before the Israelites left for the Promised Land, Moses told his people to go to the homes of the Egyptians and ask them for gold, silver, and clothes. God had made the Egyptians sympathetic, so they gave the Israelites all they asked for.

PHARAOH WHO?

Who was the Pharaoh at the time of the Exodus? Exodus does not mention Pharaoh's name, or the exact time that the Israelites left Egypt. Some historians think the Pharaoh was Ramses II. Others say it was Thutmose III. Several other names have also been suggested. In fact, no one can say for sure who he was. It's one of the mysteries in the Bible.

Why do people fear plagues?

Plagues cause widespread death, devastation, and destruction.

- One of the most famous plagues was the bubonic plague, known as the Black Death. It happened in Europe during the Middle Ages and was responsible for the death of millions of people. The disease was caused by bacteria that were spread by fleas and rats.
- A plague of some 124 billion locusts destroyed crops in the Midwest and blotted out the sun in the summer of 1874.
- In 1918, a flu epidemic killed millions worldwide. In fact, the disease killed more Americans in only a few months than were killed in World War I, World War II, and the Vietnam War combined.

The escape from Egypt is celebrated by Jews every year during the holiday of Passover. During the eight days of Passover, they cannot eat bread made with yeast. They eat a kind of flat bread, called matzo, instead, in remembrance of the escape from Egypt.

Blood Red

Red algae can turn water blood red, making it unsuitable for drinking, cooking and use in farming. In fact, one type of algae sometimes turns parts of the Gulf of Mexico red, killing thousands of fish.

Moses Rules

If you visit the United States Supreme Court building in Washington, D.C., you will see that Moses is still honored by people who help apply the laws of the country. A marble figure of Moses and two other great lawgivers are carved on the east side of the building. Moses also appears in a marble image standing with King Solomon; Zeus, the king of all Greek gods; and several other historic and mythical figures above the bench where the nine justices sit.

Journey to the Promised Land

Exodus 13–16; 19–40; Numbers 13–14

The Israelites make a dramatic escape to freedom, and after several months, arrive at the land God had promised would be theirs.

Miles and miles of desert lay before the Israelites. They gazed out at the hot sand and burning rock.

"Which way do we go?" they asked Moses.

"God will show us," Moses replied. Just then God placed a thick cloud in front of them. The cloud moved forward and the children of Israel followed. At night, God went ahead of them in the shape of a flaming fire.

Back in Egypt, Pharaoh was pacing the floor of the palace. Once again, he had changed his mind.

"I should not have let those Israelites go!" he said to his officials. "Now who will make our bricks? Who will build our buildings and our temples?"

So he gathered his army and away they rode in their best chariots, pulled by their fastest horses.

When the Israelites saw the chariots coming up behind them, they cried out in alarm. But Moses said, "Don't be afraid! Be brave, and the Lord will fight for you."

As Moses spoke, a dark cloud formed between the Israelites and the Egyptian army. The cloud made it hard for Pharaoh's men to see, but the Israelites were still in daylight.

The Israelites stopped at the edge of the Red Sea. Then God told Moses what to do. "Come!" Moses cried. "God will keep you safe." He lifted his walking stick high in the air and stretched his arm out toward the sea. A strong wind blew and caused the water to split apart. To their astonishment, the people saw a dry path form between two towering walls of water!

Moses and Aaron stepped onto the path. The frightened people found courage in their leaders. Slowly they entered the roaring sea, coaxing their animals along.

Pharaoh's army was right behind. The Israelites could hear the chariots getting closer and closer. Moses and Aaron urged the people on. Finally, everyone was safely on land. God told Moses to lift his stick again and point it toward the sea.

Immediately, the two walls of water collapsed with a tremendous crash. The whole Egyptian army was swept away.

The Israelites thanked God for using his mighty powers to save them. Moses' sister, Miriam, and the other women took out their tambourines and began to dance. Miriam gave thanks with a song:

"Sing praises to the Lord for his great victory! He has thrown the horses and their riders into the sea."

Gifts from Above

The joy and relief didn't last long. Day after day, the Israelites trudged through the desert. They started to complain to Moses and Aaron. "We wish the Lord had left us to die in Egypt. There's no food here. We're going to starve!"

But Moses told them, "The Lord will provide all the meat and bread we need."

That evening, small birds fell from the sky, sent by God to feed the hungry people.

Dew formed on the ground overnight, and in the morning the floor of the desert was covered with large flakes that looked like frost.

"What is it?" the people asked Moses.

"This is the bread that the Lord has given you to eat," he told them. "It will appear every morning so that everyone will have enough for the day."

The people gathered up the white flakes, which tasted as sweet as wafers made with honey. The Israelites called it manna.

The Ten Commandments

Two months after leaving Egypt, the Israelites came to Mount Sinai, the place where God had spoken to Moses twice before. They camped there quietly for two days. On the third morning, they were awakened by cracks of thunder and blinding bolts of lightning. The sound of trumpets echoed in the desert, and smoke covered Mount Sinai.

"What is it?" the people cried, terrified. "Moses, what is happening?"

"God has come down from the heavens," he answered.

Then the Lord called down to Moses, "Come up on the mountain, Moses. I will give you the laws my people must obey."

Moses picked up his walking stick. "Stay here and watch over the people," he told Aaron. Then he walked into the smoky cloud and disappeared.

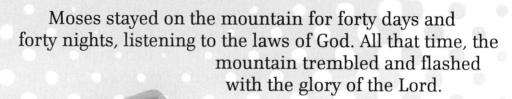

Moses stayed on the mountain for forty days and forty nights, listening to the laws of God. All that time, the mountain trembled and flashed with the glory of the Lord.

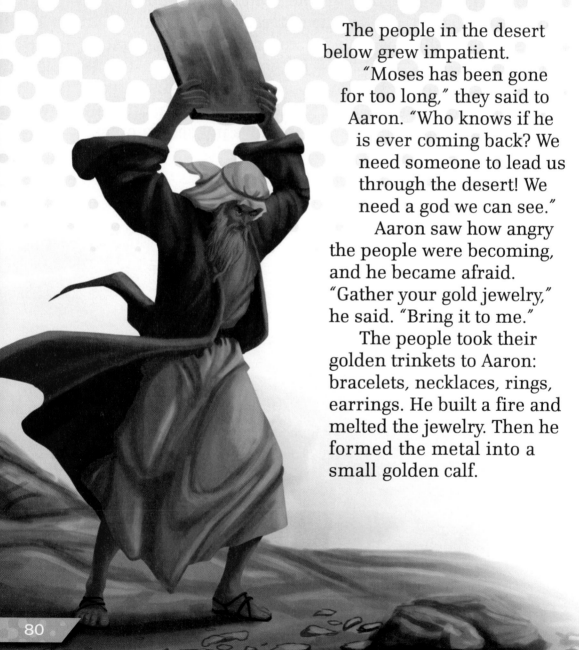

The people in the desert below grew impatient. "Moses has been gone for too long," they said to Aaron. "Who knows if he is ever coming back? We need someone to lead us through the desert! We need a god we can see."

Aaron saw how angry the people were becoming, and he became afraid. "Gather your gold jewelry," he said. "Bring it to me."

The people took their golden trinkets to Aaron: bracelets, necklaces, rings, earrings. He built a fire and melted the jewelry. Then he formed the metal into a small golden calf.

The people shouted with joy. They put the calf on an altar and began to worship it, dancing around it and singing wildly.

Soon after, Moses came down from the mountain. He was carrying two stone tablets written by the hand of God. These were the most important of God's commandments. When he saw what the people were doing, he dropped the tablets on the ground. Then he picked up each one and smashed it into a hundred pieces, crying out in fury.

"You have insulted the Lord! You don't deserve to receive his laws!" He turned to his brother. "And you, Aaron, how could you allow this to happen?"

Moses melted the golden calf and ground it into powder.

The next day he told the people, "You have done a terrible thing. I will go back to the Lord and apologize on your behalf."

God listened to Moses and said, "Tell the people to show they are ashamed of what they did. Then I will decide what to do with them."

And so the people went into mourning and prayed that God would forgive them.

God heard their prayers. He told Moses to cut two more stone tablets and bring them up to the top of Mount Sinai. Moses was there for another forty days and forty nights. Again, God wrote the laws on the tablets.

Later, the people made a special chest, called the Ark of the Covenant, to hold the tablets. They carried the Ark with them wherever they went.

A New Leader

On the twentieth day of the second month of that year, the people left Mount Sinai and began the long walk to the Promised Land—the land of Canaan that God had shown Abraham hundreds of years earlier. This was the land that God had chosen for his people, the Israelites.

When they got close to Canaan, Moses sent twelve spies ahead to explore the land of Canaan.

"Find out how many people live there and how strong they are," Moses told the men. "See if the land is good for growing crops. Now the grapes should be ripe; try to bring some back."

Forty days later, the men returned. They had brought back figs and pomegranates as well as grapes. But the men had bad news:

"The people there are strong. Some are so big that we felt like grasshoppers. And their cities are surrounded by tall walls. We could never defeat them."

But two of the leaders, Caleb and Joshua, didn't agree.

"The land is ours by right," Caleb said. "I know we can take it back!"

Joshua held up his sword. "The Lord is on our side. Those people won't have a chance against us!"

But the people were afraid. Once again, they lost faith that God would help them.

So the Lord told Moses, "Only Caleb and Joshua have shown faith in me, so only they will see the Promised Land. All the rest must wait for forty years, one for each day the land was explored."

The Israelites were left to wander from place to place.

Moses stayed with the Israelites and gave them the word of God. At last, they settled in the country of Moab.

Moses was now an old man. He knew he would not be able to lead the Israelites into the Promised Land.

So Moses called for Joshua. He placed his hands on Joshua and said, "Be strong and brave, for you must take the people across the Jordan River into Canaan. God will be with you and you will win the land that has been promised to us."

Later, Moses climbed to the top of a mountain. From there he could see the Promised Land, the land of milk and honey, a land that he would never enter.

At the age of 120, Moses died. He had spent most of his life serving God, and will forever be remembered as the man who led his people out of slavery to the land God had promised to Abraham, Issac, and Jacob.

Think about it...

Why do you think God chose Moses to lead the people out of Egypt? What qualities should you have to be a good leader?

All About the Promised Land

The Sea of Reeds

Some historians believe the Egyptian army cornered the Israelites at the "Sea of Reeds," a small marsh somewhere near the Nile Delta or farther east. Most people later thought this sea was the Red Sea, which lies between Africa and Arabia. It gets its name from the red algae in the water. No one knows for sure who is right.

WHAT DOES THE PHRASE "MANNA FROM HEAVEN" MEAN?

When people use the phrase "it was like manna from heaven," they mean that they received some unexpected help.

Idol Worship

In the ancient world, people in the Middle East worshiped many different gods. These gods were in charge of various parts of life, including weather, warfare, and farming. Worshipers would make idols, which were statues or small figures of the gods. Many believed the god was inside the idol. Once the Israelites settled in the Promised Land, they were often tempted to follow other gods, despite God's first commandment.

What Are The Ten Commandments ?

1. I am the Lord your God. Do not worship any god except me.
2. Do not make idols that look like anything in the sky or on earth. Don't bow down and worship idols.
3. Do not misuse my name.
4. Remember the Sabbath Day, to keep it holy.
5. Honor your father and your mother.
6. Do not murder.
7. Be faithful in marriage.
8. Do not steal.
9. Do not tell lies about other people.
10. Do not want anything that belongs to someone else. Do not want anyone's house, wife or husband, slaves, oxen, donkeys or anything else.

Mystery of the Ark

In the movie *Raiders of the Lost Ark*, a prop of the Ark of the Covenant was used, but the real Ark was one of the Bible's most sacred objects. The Ark was a simple chest carved out of acacia wood and gold. The box was about 4 feet (122 cm) wide, 27 inches (69 cm) long, and 27 inches (69 cm) deep. The lid on the chest was known as the "mercy" seat and was the place on which God said he would rest. The last time anyone saw the Ark was around 587 B.C. That's when the Babylonians invaded Jerusalem.

The Walls of Jericho

Joshua 1–6

Moses chose Joshua to be the one to lead the Israelites to the Promised Land. Joshua has faith that God will show him what to do.

Joshua watched as his two spies came up the hill. He had sent them out to scout the land of Canaan—the very land God had promised to give the people of Israel. In particular, Joshua wanted to know about the city of Jericho, whose great walls he could see towering in the distance.

"Well," Joshua said, "what did you find out?"

"Good news!" the spies said. "God will certainly give

us this land, for the people in the city are terrified of us."

Joshua nodded, but he knew there were still problems to overcome. As the new leader of the Israelites, it was up to him to win this battle and bring the people into the Promised Land. His people needed to cross the raging waters of the flooded Jordan River. Then they needed to get inside those walls around Jericho. How could they ever do it? Joshua was afraid.

As Joshua thought about this, he remembered the words God spoke to him as the people had approached the Promised Land. "Be strong," God had told him. "Do not be afraid and do not give up. The Lord your God is with you wherever you go."

Early the next morning, the people got ready to break camp and cross the roaring Jordan. An excited buzz filled the camp. "Did you hear? God has spoken to Joshua," the people told each other. "The Lord is going to do great wonders among us."

With the instructions God had given him still fresh in his mind, Joshua spoke to the priests: "Today you will know that the living God is among you. You will have no trouble driving out the people now living in this land. The Ark of the Covenant, which belongs to the Lord, will lead us across the river."

The priests lifted the wooden chest containing the stone tablets engraved with the Ten Commandments and walked to the river bank. Then Joshua gave the command, "Step into the river."

As soon as the priests' feet touched the river's edge, the water stopped flowing! The river bed was completely dry! The priests stood with the Ark in the middle as they watched everyone cross over safely.

The Israelites were joyous after safely crossing the Jordan River. They were one step closer to claiming the Promised Land!

Now their next challenge loomed ahead of them—the great walls of Jericho. The gates were shut tightly because, just as the spies had said, the people were terrified of them. They were even more afraid after hearing how God had stopped the flood waters of the Jordan to let the people cross.

Once again, the Lord gave Joshua the battle plan. "Tell your army to march around the city once a day for six days. Seven priests will walk ahead of the Ark, carrying trumpets. On the seventh day, the priests will again march around the city seven times, but this time they will blow their trumpets as they march.

"Then," God said, "when the people hear one long blast on the horns, they are to give a mighty shout."

Joshua followed God's instructions exactly. On the first morning, the army gathered behind the Ark of the Covenant and the seven priests carrying trumpets. As they marched around the walls of the city, the priests blew their horns. What a noise they made!

Each day, for the next six days, the army of Israel got up and marched around the city of Jericho, with the priests blowing their horns.

On the seventh day, all the Israelites got up at dawn and began to march around the city. Once, twice, three times, until they had circled the city seven times.

On the seventh time around, the priests sounded a long blast on their horns.

"Shout!" cried Joshua. "For the Lord has given you the city."

A great cry went up from the people. They shouted as loudly as they could. And then, to the amazement of everyone, the walls of Jericho came crashing down!

The Israelites charged into the city from all sides. At the end of the battle, the city was theirs.

The news quickly spread throughout the land that the Lord was with Joshua, and his name became famous.

Think about it...

Sometimes we have a big problem that seems impossible to solve, like the Walls of Jericho. What can you learn from this story that might help you find an answer?

All About
Joshua and Jericho

Blow Your Horn

Trumpets in those days were made from the horns of rams. The insides of the horns were scraped out to make a hollow tube. Today, ram's horns are still used in Jewish temples to call the people to worship. They are called shofars.

The Walls of Jericho

The city of Jericho was built on a huge mound of earth, which formed a hill. That's why the Bible says the people had to go up into the city. On top of this hill was a stone wall about 15 feet high. On top of that was a mud brick wall about six feet thick, and another 20 to 26 feet high. All together, from the base of the hill to the very top, the walls of Jericho stood 46 feet high! That's about the height of a four or five-story building!

A Secret Weapon

While the cities of Canaan had strong walls and large armies, Joshua and the Israelites had a secret weapon on their side—God!

- Once, during a battle against the kings of five different countries, God helped the Israelites by throwing the enemy into such a panic that they killed each other in the confusion.
- God caused a great hailstorm to fall on enemy soldiers who were trying to run away. More were killed by hailstorm than by the sword.
- In answer to Joshua's prayer, God made the sun and moon stand still over a battlefield so Joshua's men would have enough light to round up and destroy all their enemies. The Bible tells us that the sun stopped in the heavens for almost twenty-four hours!

WORLD RECORDS

- Jericho was the first city conquered by Joshua and the Israelites as they moved into Canaan.
- It is the lowest city in the world, located 1,000 feet below sea level.
- It is the oldest city that has been continually inhabited. People have been living in and around Jericho for 11,000 years!

Who was living in the city of Jericho?

Descendants of Noah's son, Ham, had lived in the land for hundreds of years before Joshua and the Israelites arrived. They were famous as merchants and seamen and were known for their artistic skill. They worshiped many gods. One was the sun-god, Baal.

DID YOU KNOW?

Jericho was known as "the city of palm trees" because of all the trees that were fed by its many fresh water springs.

The Story of Samson

Judges 13–16

After Joshua had led the Israelites to the Promised Land, the people loved and honored God. But as time passed, they stopped obeying God's laws. God sent an enemy who took over the land. The people suffered for many years at the hand of a cruel ruler. Finally, God took pity on them. He sent a hero to destroy the enemy and return the land to the Israelites. That hero was Samson.

Of all the young men in the tribe of Dan, Samson was the most admired. For one thing, he had long, long hair that he wore in seven braids down his back. He was also very brave and very strong.

Samson's parents had raised their son according to rules they had been given by an angel of the Lord. One of those rules was that Samson could never cut his hair. The hair would be a symbol of his devotion to God, and it would be the source of his great strength.

Samson's parents had remained faithful to God when few others did. So God had blessed them with an extraordinary son who grew up to be the strongest man anyone had ever seen. He could move boulders by himself, lift a donkey over his head, and carry a tree trunk across his shoulders. Once, when Samson was attacked by a lion, he grabbed the beast and killed it with his bare hands. Even the cruel Philistines who ruled the land were afraid of him.

Samson grew older, and every year he became stronger. Soon, the people saw him as a great leader. They listened to his words and did whatever he demanded of them. The Philistines saw his power grow. They tried many times to capture him, but Samson was too strong.

But then, one day, Samson met Delilah.

Delilah was a beautiful woman who lived in the Valley of Sorek. Samson fell in love with her at first sight. He forgot about his home and forgot about his tribe. He wanted only to be with Delilah.

The Philistine leaders heard what was going on. Here, finally, was a way for them to destroy the man who frightened them so much! They sent for Delilah and made her an offer.

"Find out the secret of his strength," they said to her, "and we will pay you eleven hundred shekels of silver." Delilah gasped. Eleven hundred shekels! That was a fortune! Within moments, she agreed to do what they asked.

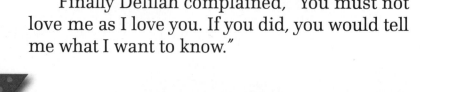

The next time Samson came to see her, Delilah tried to wheedle the secret out of him. She knew he liked to be flattered.

"Oh, Samson," she said. "I am such a lucky woman. You are so kind, and so brave. And you're the strongest man I have ever seen. Tell me, please... What is the secret of your strength?"

Samson laughed and shook his head. "I can't tell you that."

Day after day, Delilah tried to get him to tell her the secret. Day after day, Samson refused.

Finally Delilah complained, "You must not love me as I love you. If you did, you would tell me what I want to know."

Samson couldn't bear to make her angry. "Do you see my hair, how long it is? It is one way I show my devotion to God. If my hair were cut, my strength would leave me."

Delilah smiled and kissed him. But that night, she went to see one of the Philistine rulers. He gave her the silver coins. Later, as Samson slept with his head in her lap, the man came in and cut off his seven braids. When Samson awoke, he found himself bound with a dozen strong ropes. He roared with anger, but he could not break free. His great strength was gone.

Philistine soldiers came to drag him off to prison. Samson was thrown in a dark cell, and the soldiers put out his eyes. Blind and weak, he remained a prisoner for a long time. But the Philistines forgot one thing. They forgot to keep cutting his hair.

Months later, the Philistine rulers decided to have a great feast in honor of their god, Dagon, to thank him for delivering the leader of the Israelites. Thousands would come to the celebration, and a sacrifice would be made to the god.

Then one of the Philistines had an idea.

"Let us bring Samson to the temple, so that the people can see for themselves how weak he is. It will be great entertainment!" The others agreed enthusiastically.

So Samson was brought from his cell. His legs were shackled, and he shuffled when he walked. A boy led him into the temple, and the crowd began laughing and pointing. Samson heard them. He bowed his head.

"Take me to the main pillars at the center of the temple," he said to the boy. "I am weak and tired. I need something to lean against."

The boy smirked. The great Samson needed a pillar to lean on! But he did as Samson asked, and the crowd laughed even louder.

"Look at the leader of the Israelites! He can't even stand up on his own!"

Samson listened to the laughter for a few moments more. Then, suddenly, he straightened. Once more, he stood strong and tall. He placed his hands against the two pillars and pushed with all his might.

"Oh, God," he cried, "let me die with the Philistines!" The pillars toppled and the temple came crashing down, burying the thousands who had come to mock him.

Samson was a hero. He had freed his people from the rule of the Philistines.

Think about it...

Samson gave up his life to save his people. What heroic acts have you seen and admired?

All About Samson

A Special Kind of Guy

Think you have a lot of rules to follow? Samson was a Nazarite. Nazarites were special people set apart to serve God. As a Nazarite, Samson could not:

- drink wine or any other strong drink;
- eat grapes;
- visit a grave or touch the dead;
- cut his hair (Whoops!).

WHAT'S IN A NAME?

Samson's name comes from the Hebrew word *Shamesh*, which means "sun." God was also known as "a sun and shield." So Samson's name seems to connect him strongly to God.

Who Were the Philistines?

No one is quite sure! Many scholars think they came from Crete. Others think they began as roving bands of pirates. But they entered Canaan as invaders and conquerors, occupying the coastal strip of southwestern Canaan. Their five great capital cities were Gaza, Ashkelon, Ashdod, Ekron, and Gath. Samson was born to the tribe of Dan, which had settled in the hills a little to the northwest of Jerusalem.

DID YOU KNOW?

The term "Philistine" is still used today! But now, it refers to someone who has no interest in arts and culture.

How Long Was Samson's Hair?

On average, hair grows about 6 inches a year, though not as quickly for very young children. But this still means that between the ages of 5 and 20, Samson's hair could have grown to more than 7 feet! Most hair breaks when it reaches a certain length, but Samson always had a lot of 'strong' in his long locks.

Dagon was an idol with the body of a fish and the head and hands of a man.

You Don't Mess with Samson!

Why? Here are just a few of the things this biblical superman did when he got angry. He:

• tore apart a lion with his bare hands;
• killed 100 men with the jawbone of an ass;
• carried the city gates of Gaza to the top of a high hill near the city of Hebron. That's a distance of about 40 miles (64 km).
• destroyed the temple of Dagon by pushing against its two main supporting pillars.

The Story of Ruth

Ruth 1–4

Ruth was a brave and loyal woman who became the great-grandmother of Israel's greatest king, King David. This story tells how Ruth came from a faraway land to make her home with her mother-in-law's people in Bethlehem.

Naomi put down the shirt she had been mending. "I wish we could go back to Bethlehem," she said to her husband, Elimelech. "I miss my friends and family."

"It's no use dreaming," her husband replied. "We're doing much better here in Moab, where the land is good, and we have plenty to eat."

Elimelech had moved his wife and two sons from their homeland, Judah, to the country of Moab after his crops had failed. But they were not happy there.

The people of Moab had different beliefs. They didn't worship the God of Abraham, Isaac, and Jacob. They believed in many different gods, so Elimelech's family had to pretend to worship the gods, too. But God Almighty was with them in their hearts.

Naomi sighed. Then she picked up her sewing and went back to work.

Time passed. Both of their sons married women from Moab. Naomi loved her two daughters-in-law—Orpah and Ruth. They loved her in return. They talked with her, worked with her, and laughed with her.

But within ten years, Elimelech and both his sons died.

Now all three women were widows.

The three women lived together for a long time. Then one day, Naomi came rushing into the house with great news.

"There are crops growing everywhere in Judah. Now I can go back to Bethlehem and be with my people again."

Ruth and Orpah wanted to go with her, and soon they started on their way, with a donkey to carry all their belongings.

As they walked along, Naomi began to think about her daughters-in-law. Both were young enough to marry again, but she knew that not many men in Judah would want to marry a woman from Moab.

"My daughters," Naomi said, "I love you and thank you for wanting to come with me. But you are young and should marry again. You'll have a better chance of finding husbands if you stay here."

"No," Ruth said. "I will go with you."

"I will also go," said Orpah.

Naomi tried to get them to change their minds.

"Just think," she said. "I have relatives in Bethlehem who will look after me. But you will grow old with no husbands to provide for you. You will be lonely and poor."

Orpah cried and kissed her mother-in-law. "Good-bye, then," she said. "I will never forget you." She turned and went back the way they had come.

Ruth made no move to go.

"Go on," Naomi begged, with tears in her eyes. "You must go with her."

But Ruth said, "Please don't tell me to leave you and return home! I will go where you go. I will live where you live; your people will be my people, your God will be my God."

Naomi could see that Ruth had made up her mind. "Bless you," she whispered.

The two women walked on.

When they arrived in Bethlehem, Naomi led Ruth to the house where she had lived before.

At dinner time, Naomi picked up the sack holding grain they would use to make the bread. It was almost empty.

"Tomorrow I will go into the fields. The farmers here always leave some grain at the edges of their fields." Naomi said. "It is the law. Anyone who needs it may come and take some away."

"Let me go," Ruth said, "I will be able to carry more."

And so the next morning, Ruth went out to find a barley field. After a while, she came to a field with plenty of grain and joined some other women there. The field belonged to Boaz, a rich and important man.

Ruth Meets Boaz

As it happened, Boaz was in the fields that day.

"Who is that young woman?" Boaz said, pointing to Ruth.

His foreman said, "That is Ruth, who just arrived in Bethlehem with Naomi."

"Oh," said Boaz, "I have heard the story. She would not leave her mother-in-law, even though it meant coming to a strange land."

Boaz walked over to Ruth.

"You have been very kind to Naomi," he said. "I pray the Lord God of Israel will reward you for what you have done. Please take as much grain as you want. If you get thirsty, drink from these water jars."

At lunch time, he invited Ruth to sit with him and his workers. He gave her more food than she could eat. When she returned to the field, Boaz watched her leave. He told his men to let her take some of the better stalks of barley.

"Whose field did you work in?" Naomi asked when Ruth showed her the large basket of grain. "God bless the man who treated you so well."

"It was Boaz," Ruth said. "Do you know him?"

"Boaz! Yes, he is a close relative and a good man. He is one of the men who will be taking care of the business that my husband used to tend to."

Ruth returned to Boaz's field every day, and every day Boaz watched her and spoke to her. He began to care deeply for this kind, lovely young woman.

Naomi saw that Boaz would be a good husband for Ruth. She knew how she could arrange it.

Naomi went to Boaz and told him that she wanted to sell some land that her husband had owned. According to law, whoever bought the land would have to marry Ruth. Perhaps Boaz would buy it!

Boaz listened to Naomi's request, but he was troubled. For it was also the law that the closest relative would be given the first chance to buy any property in the family. There was another relative ahead of Boaz, so he went to see the man.

"Do you want to buy Naomi's land?" Boaz asked him.

"Yes!" the man answered. "It is good land and I would be happy to purchase it."

"Good," Boaz said. The two men took off their sandals and traded with each other. That meant that the deal had been made.

Then Boaz added, "You know if you buy the land, you must marry Ruth. Then if you have a son, the property will stay in the family."

"Marry the foreigner?" the man said. "Then no. I don't want the land." He took back his sandals and walked away.

This was just what Boaz had hoped would happen. He had fallen in love with Ruth. Now he could marry her! He rushed off to tell Naomi.

As it happened, Ruth was as happy as Boaz. They were married, and by the next year they had a baby boy. He was called Obed, which means "one who worships."

Think about it...

Why do you think Ruth was willing to give up everything to stay with Naomi? In what ways can you show that you are loyal to your friends?

All About Ruth

Where in the Desert was Moab?

Moab was located east of the Dead Sea in what is today Jordan. People who lived in Moab were called the Moabites. They were relatives of Lot, the nephew of Abraham. Although related to the Hebrews, the Moabites were often at war with the Israelites.

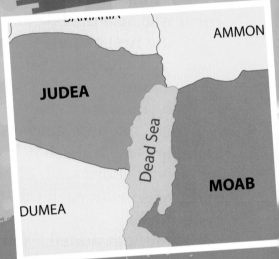

Down on the Farm

Hebrew farmers in Bethlehem harvested grain by cutting the stalks with sickles or by pulling the plants up by the roots. They then spread the stalks out on a threshing floor. Oxen and cattle walked over the stalks to separate the seeds from the plant. Women then ground the grain into flour using heavy stones. Farmers often left grain along the side of the fields for poor people to glean, or gather.

The Importance of Ruth

Ruth and Boaz had a son named Obed. Obed was the father of Jesse, and Jesse was the father of King David. That makes Ruth the great-grandmother of Israel's most beloved king, who was an ancestor of Jesus.

Ruth   Boaz

Obed

Jesse

King David

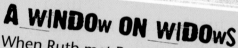
A WINDOW ON WIDOWS

When Ruth met Boaz, women in Israel could not own property or run a business. This made life hard for widows like Ruth and Naomi. They had to depend on men in the family for food and shelter. Many widows lived in poverty.

Harvest Festival

One of the most important Jewish festivals occurs each year at the end of the grain harvest. Known as Sukkoth, Jews honor Ruth during the festival by reading her story.

The "Orpah Show"

The mother of the TV celebrity, Oprah Winfrey, had originally named her daughter Orpah, after the daughter-in-law who decided not to stay with Naomi. However, on Winfrey's birth certificate, someone had switched the "r" and "p" to "Oprah."

David and Goliath

1 Samuel 17

When he was just a young boy, David was chosen by God to be the second king of Israel. Even then David was very brave.

David looked up the hill and sighed. He was tired from his long walk, and so was his donkey. The donkey, loaded with sacks of roasted wheat, bread, and cheese, suddenly came to a stop. David tugged on the lead. "Come on!" he said. "We're almost there."

David's father had asked him to deliver the supplies to his brothers who were camped with King Saul's army.

When they finally reached the top of the hill, David saw, spread out in the valley below, the tents of the armies of Israel and the Philistines. David moved quickly toward Israel's camp, where he spotted his older brothers among the soldiers. He called out to them: "Eliab! Abinadab! Shammah!"

The men turned at the sound of David's voice, but, before they had time to speak, another voice boomed out from the camp of the enemy. David turned around and saw a terrifying sight. A giant soldier stood in the valley between the two camps, waving his sword at the Israelites and calling out to them.

"You are all cowards! You are afraid to send someone to fight me!"

Then the giant laughed.

"Who is that?" David asked.

"He is called Goliath," a soldier answered. "He comes out every day and challenges us. But no one wants to fight him—he's too big."

David stared at the giant. "Who does he think he is? He's making fun of the army of God!"

Goliath roared, "Why are you afraid? I'll take on your champion, your best man. Whoever wins the fight will win the battle."

David saw the Israelites backing away.

"Stop!" he yelled to the retreating soldiers. What was wrong with them? Didn't they understand that they wouldn't be fighting alone? Didn't they know God would be with them?

"Won't anyone stand up to this Goliath?" David asked. "If none of you will—I'll fight him!"

When David's older brothers heard that, they became angry.

"Who do you think you are?" Eliab asked. "That giant could crush your skull with a single blow."

"No, he can't," said David. "And I know I can win because God is with me."

"Be quiet," said David's brother. "Someone will hear you bragging."

Someone did hear, and almost before David knew what was happening, soldiers led him straight to King Saul.

King Saul looked down at David and smiled. "Just how would you go about fighting Goliath?" he asked. "You're just a boy."

David stood tall and answered, "My King, I care for my father's sheep. When a lion or a bear drags a sheep away, I go after the beast and kill it. If the Lord can rescue me from fierce animals, he can keep me safe when I fight Goliath."

King Saul was impressed by David's courage. "All right," he said. "You can fight. But I think you'd better wear my armor."

Servants fastened a thick metal breastplate on David. They buckled on a heavy belt. They handed David a huge shield to protect him from the blows of Goliath's sword. In David's other hand, they placed a sword that weighed David down so much that he almost dropped it on the ground.

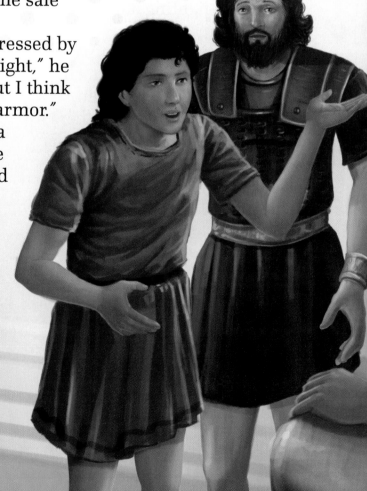

Finally, they put Saul's helmet on David's head.

The armor was so heavy that he could hardly move. So, piece by piece, off came the king's armor. David would fight Goliath with only his faith in God for protection.

David picked up his shepherd's stick and slingshot and left the king's tent. He walked straight to the small stream in the bottom of the valley and picked up five round, smooth stones. He tucked them into his leather bag and then started up the hill toward Goliath.

When Goliath saw David, he laughed so loudly that David was sure people could hear him in Bethlehem. "What does your king think I am? A dog? Is that why he has sent a child here to fight me, armed with only a stick?" Goliath was in a rage. "When I'm finished with you, I'll feed you to the birds and wild animals."

David stood calmly. He said, "You come to fight me with a sword, a spear, and a dagger. I come to fight you in the name of the Lord God All-Powerful—the God of Israel's army. You will be sorry you insulted him. Then the whole world will know that my God is real."

David put a smooth stone into his slingshot. Goliath drew his weapon and raised it high in the air. David waited ... and waited ... until Goliath charged forward.

David raised his arm and swung his slingshot in circles over his head: *Whirr, whirr, whirr!* Then David let the stone fly!

The stone struck Goliath in the middle of the forehead. He staggered, sank to his knees, and tumbled face down on the ground. The mighty giant was dead.

For a moment, the armies on both sides of the valley stood in stunned silence. Then the Israelites grabbed their swords and began to chase the Philistine army. The Philistines were terrified and ran away, crying out in fear.

After the battle was over, David walked into King Saul's tent carrying the head of their dreaded enemy. King Saul stood beside David and said, "Look at this shepherd boy who has shown great courage—and who has shown us all the power of the God of Israel!"

Think about it...

Everyone faces giant problems in life, and those giant problems require courage. What do you think courage is? How did David learn courage?

All About
David and Goliath

A Gigantic Problem

So, how big was Goliath? Most Bible experts think he was more than nine feet tall. That's one yardstick taller than a tall man of six feet! It's even taller than the tallest basketball players and biggest football players.
Goliath was so strong he could wear chest armor that weighed 125 pounds. He could also handle a spear that was so big that the spearhead alone weighed more than 15 pounds.
No wonder no one wanted to tangle with Goliath!

Singing for a King

After David killed Goliath, King Saul asked him to live in his house. He treated him like a son. David had a small harp, called a lyre. Saul liked to listen to David play the lyre and sing.

NOT JUST A SINGER

Do you know the Book of Psalms? Many psalms are songs that praise God and the beauty of God's earth. There are 150 psalms in the Bible. Guess who wrote 73 of them? David! He wrote his psalms after he became king to show his thanks for God's love and protection.

How did he do it?

You might be wondering how David could kill a huge giant with just a slingshot. Well, in Bible times, a sling was considered to be a very deadly weapon. In fact, some soldiers were especially trained to use the sling! A sling typically had two straps that formed a pouch, often made of woven goat hair. The shooter would whirl the sling above his head as fast as he could, and then let go of one of the straps. The stone would fly out of the pouch like a speeding bullet.

King David

When he was a young boy, David was chosen by God to be king after Saul died. David became Israel's greatest king. His army defeated the Philistines, and he established the capital city of Jerusalem.

DID YOU KNOW?

Even today, when we talk about a person or group taking on a much bigger and stronger opponent, we call it a "David and Goliath" story.

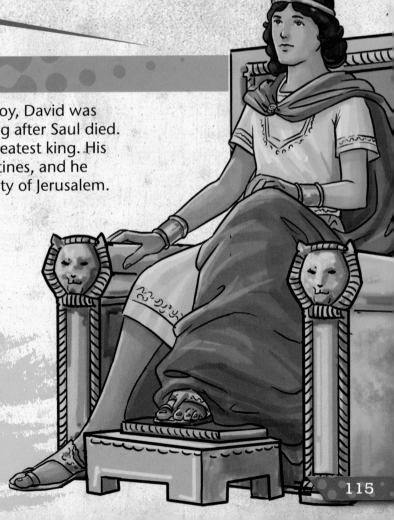

115

The Wise King Solomon

1 Kings 3–4

David's son, Solomon, became the third king of Israel.

King Solomon was a very wise man. Every day, people came to him with questions that needed answers or problems that needed to be solved. Solomon's wisdom was a gift promised by God when Solomon first became king.

Solomon's father, David, had been a brave and much loved king. David had been chosen by God to lead his people—a nation so great, there were too many to count. With God's help, David had defeated the enemies of Israel and set up his government in Jerusalem.

After David died, God gave his blessing to Solomon as the next king. But Solomon was worried.

"My father was a great king," he thought. "How am I ever going to take his place?"

One night, God came to Solomon in a dream and said, "Solomon, ask for anything you want and I will give it to you."

Solomon replied, "Lord God, you have made me king, but I am very young and know so little about being a leader. Please make me wise and teach me the difference between right and wrong."

God was very pleased with this answer. Not only did he agree to give Solomon great knowledge about many things, but he also promised to give him riches and honor as well.

All this came to pass, and now Solomon was the richest and wisest man in Israel.

One day, two women were brought to see the king. They were having a loud argument.

"The child is mine!" screamed one woman.

"No, he's my son!" cried the other.

On and on the two women argued, back and forth, until the king raised his hand.

"Silence!" he commanded. A hush fell over the crowded courtroom. The only sound was the crying of the baby lying in a basket between the two women. All eyes were on King Solomon. What was he going to do? How was he going to decide who was the real mother of the baby boy?

"Please, my king," said the first woman. "This woman and I live in the same house. I gave birth to a baby while she was in the house with me—a beautiful baby boy. This woman had a child, too, about three days later. But her baby died in the night. So she came and took my baby from me and put her baby in my arms. When I woke up, I thought my baby was dead. But it wasn't him!"

The other woman spoke up, "Of course, it was your son. My baby is lying right there!"

"No," sobbed the first woman. "My baby is living. Yours is dead!"

And the two began to shout back and forth again.

"Silence!" the king ordered again. "Here is what I have heard. You both claim the living child is yours, and each says that the dead child belongs to the other."

The women nodded silently.

"All right then," said the king. "Bring me a sword."

An attendant came forward with the sword. The entire court held its breath as they waited to see what the king would do.

"Since both women claim this boy, cut the living child in two and give half to each," he commanded.

The first woman cried out, "No, no, my Lord. Don't do that. Give her the child—please don't kill him."

But the other woman said, "Fine. He will neither be yours nor mine. Go ahead and divide the child."

Then King Solomon said, "Do not kill the child, but give him to the woman who wanted to save him. She is his real mother."

Everyone in the court let out a sigh of relief. Only King Solomon could have made such a wise decision.

Think about it...

If you had a chance to ask God for anything, what would you ask for? Why? Do you think Solomon made a good choice? Why, or why not?

All About King Solomon

Smarter than the Average King

When it came to wisdom, King Solomon was the wisest of the wise. He wrote 3,000 proverbs and more than 1,000 songs. He knew about all kinds of plants and animals. In fact, kings from all over the world sent people to Jerusalem to learn from Solomon. One visitor was the Queen of Sheba. She traveled from her home in Arabia to Israel to find out for herself if Solomon was really as wise as everyone said. She asked him one difficult question after another. To the queen's amazement, he answered every one correctly!

Proverbs are clever, easy-to-remember sayings that give good advice about things such as how to stay out of trouble and how to live the right way.

DID YOU KNOW?

Every three years, King Solomon sent his ships across the sea to bring back monkeys and peacocks from a far off land called Ophir.

A King's Ransom

King Solomon controlled major trade routes through Israel and made 666 talents (25 tons) of gold a year from taxes paid by traders to use these roads. He owned a stable of 12,000 horses and 1,400 chariots. He drank from gold cups and wore robes woven of the finest cloth. His throne was made of ivory and covered with pure gold. He was the richest man who ever lived.

Gold nuggets were used to pay taxes.

A Preview of Proverbs

"If you are already wise, you will become even wiser. And if you are smart, you will learn to understand."

"Children with good sense make their parents happy, but foolish children make them sad."

"Laziness leads to poverty; hard work makes you rich."

Home for the Ark

It took 20 years for King Solomon to build his grand temple, located on the site of the Temple Mount in present-day Jerusalem. For many centuries, Solomon's Temple housed a wooden box that contained the Ten Commandments.

The Courage of Esther

Esther 2–8

Esther makes a promise to her cousin. She doesn't know that this promise will someday cause great danger to her people.

The king of Persia wanted a wife. But King Xerxes did not want just any woman. He wanted someone who was beautiful, intelligent, and kind. So he ordered his officials to bring the loveliest of the young, unmarried women in his kingdom to the palace. They would live there for a year, being taught and groomed by members of the king's court. Finally, the king would choose his queen from among them.

One of the palace officials heard of the king's plan and began to worry. The man's name was Mordecai. Mordecai had a beautiful young cousin, Esther, whom he had raised as his daughter and loved very much. He knew that she would be one of the young women chosen to live in the palace.

"If I am chosen, then I will go," said Esther. "Please don't worry, Cousin. I'm sure King Xerxes is a good man."

"That may be true," said Mordecai. "But never forget that we are Jews, and that my great-grandfather was one of the thousands who came to this country as a captive. Even today, we have many enemies among the Persian people. So promise me, Esther—promise me that you will not tell anyone you are my cousin, or that you are a Jew."

Esther promised. Then, just as Mordecai had predicted, the king's officials chose Esther as well as several other women.

The year went by swiftly. Every day, the young women learned how to look and act like a queen.

During that year, Esther became a favorite among the women and among those who watched over them. Her laughter made everyone smile. Her kindness touched their hearts. Esther was wise. She was able to solve problems and end disputes with a few thoughtful words.

Finally, it was time to meet the king. Each woman dressed in her finest silks and applied the oils and perfumes she had been taught to use. One by one, they presented themselves to Xerxes. But the moment the king saw Esther, he stopped his search. Xerxes placed a crown on her head and made her his queen. Soon, he loved her with all his heart.

Mordecai continued to work in the palace, watching over Esther from a distance. One day, he overheard two of the king's officers muttering to each other.

"We will never gain the power we deserve while this pompous fool, Xerxes, sits on the throne," said one.

"But what can we do? He is the king!"

"Yes. But there are men who will do anything for a price."

Mordecai crept silently away. He found Esther and told her about the plot to kill Xerxes.

"I will get word to the king at once," said Esther. "And Cousin, I will tell him who it was that saved his life."

Esther did as she had said. The two officers were arrested and hanged on the gallows. Mordecai's deed was recorded in a special book that told the history of the king. Despite this, the king quickly forgot about him.

In fact, not long afterwards, Xerxes promoted someone else to the highest position in his kingdom. His name was Haman, and he was proud and very vain. But the king did not know this. Xerxes ordered everyone in his kingdom to honor Haman by kneeling down to him whenever he passed by. Everyone obeyed—except for Mordecai.

"But why?" asked some of the other officials. "You are putting yourself in great danger."

"Haman's people, the Amalekites, have always been enemies of the Jews, and Haman himself hates us. I will never kneel before him."

And he didn't. Whenever Haman appeared, Mordecai stood up even straighter. Haman became enraged.

How dare this Jew show such disrespect! he thought. *I want him dead, him and all his people!*

But Haman did not have the power to order the execution of the Jews. He would have to convince the king that the Jews were a danger to his kingdom. It didn't take him long to come up with a plan. He went to see Xerxes.

"Your Majesty," he said. "There are a few people in this kingdom who are not like the rest of us. They have different customs, and some of them even refuse to obey your laws! My advice, O King, is that we get rid of them before they can poison others with their ways."

Haman's news disturbed Xerxes. He gave Haman his official ring and said, "Do what you will with these people."

Haman wasted no time. He sent out a decree that on the thirteenth day of the twelfth month, the king's soldiers would be sent out to kill all the Jews in the land. And Haman had a special gallows built where Mordecai would be hanged.

Mordecai was horrified. He had been willing to risk his own life, but he never thought that Haman would kill innocent people as well.

He went to find one of Esther's servants.

"You must go to the queen," Mordecai said. "Take her a copy of the decree so that she knows what Haman is doing. Ask her to plead with the king to save us."

When Esther got the message, she turned pale. "What Haman is planning is monstrous! But no one, not even I, may go before the king unless he commands it. To do so can mean death!"

The servant nodded. "Your cousin knows this. And he said to tell you: only you can save your people."

A sudden calm came over Esther. "He is right, of course. I will go to the king, and if he orders my death, so be it. "

Esther put on her royal robes and went to the king's inner court. He looked up in surprise when she entered, and Esther held her breath. But then the king smiled.

"My lovely queen," he said. "What is it you would like? Whatever you ask, it is yours."

Esther smiled in return. "For now, I ask only that you come tonight to a special dinner I have prepared. Bring Haman as well."

"As you wish," said the king.

When Haman heard the news, he was overjoyed. He alone, of all the officials of the court, had been asked to dine with the king and queen!

That night, on his way to the dining hall, Haman once again passed by Mordecai. Still, the man refused to kneel. Haman's anger flared, but he calmed himself. "Soon," he muttered.

The meal was magnificent. There was fine wine, delicious fruit, and the best meats.

After Haman had left, Esther said to the king, "I have another request, my lord. Come tomorrow to another dinner I will prepare, and I will tell you what it is."

The king agreed, wondering what his queen was planning. That night, he couldn't sleep. He had a servant read to him from the records of all that had happened since he had been king. When the servant read of how Mordecai had once saved the king's life, he sat up in his bed.

"What has been done to reward Mordecai for this great deed?"

"Why, nothing, Your Majesty," said his servant.

So the next day, the king called for Haman.

"What should I do for a man I wish to honor?" asked the king.

Thinking the king could only mean him, Haman said, "I would have a high official place one of the king's own robes on this man. Then the official should lead the man through the streets on one of the king's best horses, crying, 'This is how the king honors a man!'"

"Excellent," said the king. "This is what I want you to do for Mordecai, the Jew, who once saved my life. Do it immediately."

Haman was stunned, but he had no choice but to obey. He led Mordecai through the streets on a fine horse, shouting out the very words he had suggested to the king. Then he went home, his face burning in shame. But he comforted himself, knowing that the man he hated would soon be dead.

That night's feast was even more magnificent than the first. When everyone had finished eating, the king turned to Esther.

"And now, my wife. Will I finally hear your request?"

Esther stood, walked over to the king, then knelt at his feet. "Only this. I ask that you save my life and that of my people. I am a Jew, cousin to Mordecai, and an order has been given that we and all our people must die."

The king was not upset about the secret that Esther had kept, but he was furious about the terrible order. "Who would dare! Who gave this order?"

Esther pointed to Haman. "This man, my king. It is Haman who has done this."

Haman cowered before the king and queen.

"Wait," he said. "Please. I didn't know...."

But the king's anger was too great. He canceled the awful decree Haman had tricked him into writing. And he ordered that Haman be hanged—on the very gallows he had built for Mordecai.

All over the land, the Jewish people rejoiced.

Brave, wise Esther had saved them.

Think about it...

Esther risked her life to save her people. What would you be willing to risk for others?

All About Esther

Captives

Mordecai, Esther, and all the Jews who lived in Persia at this time were the grandchildren and great-grandchildren of people who had lived in the city of Jerusalem. A hundred years earlier, King Nebuchadnezzar of Babylonia had destroyed the Holy Temple in that city and had captured the brightest and most talented Jews and taken them to Babylonia in the Persian Empire.

DID YOU KNOW?

The Book of Esther is the only book in the Bible that doesn't mention God by name!

Queen Superstar

Esther had two names. Her parents had given her the Hebrew name, *Hadassah,* which means myrtle tree. When she was introduced at the royal court, she was given the Persian name Esther, which means star. The king had two names, too. Xerxes [zerk-cees] is his Persian name. The Hebrews called him Ahasuerus [A-ha-zer-us].

Myrtle tree

All of these countries were part of the Persian Empire

Welcome to Persia

The nation of Persia was part of the vast Persian Empire. In fact, some people who live in Iran still speak the Persian language. The first mention of Persians dates back to the 9th century BC. The Jews' history in Persia goes back to the 6th century BC, and today about 25,000 Jews still live in Iran.

MAKE SOME NOISE!

Do you want to have some fun? Visit a Jewish temple and celebrate the holiday of Purim. The Book of Esther, called the *megillah*, is read aloud on that holiday. It's not just a reading, though—every time Haman's name is mentioned, the congregation shouts, boos, and uses graggers, a special type of hand-held noisemaker, to make a deafening noise. After the reading, you might get to eat *hamantaschen*, cookies that are shaped like triangles. *Hamanstaschen* means "Haman's pockets."

Have a Party!

People—especially kids—also dress up in costumes and have parties on Purim. This tradition dates back more than 400 years!

Jonah and the Fish

Jonah 1–4

Jonah learns that God is all-forgiving, even to the enemies of Israel.

The storm raged and roared, tossing the wooden ship as if it were a twig.

"Watch out!" a sailor yelled above the howling wind. *Crash!* The mast hit the deck.

"In all the years I've sailed this sea, I've never seen a storm like this," said one of his shipmates.

Sailors scrambled around the deck of the ship, first tying things down, then throwing the cargo overboard.

One sailor suddenly had an idea. "That stranger who came onboard this morning – that Jonah ... the storm began almost at the moment his feet touched the deck. Where is he?"

Several sailors lunged down the steps and into the hold where they woke up Jonah who had been sleeping for hours. The sailors brought him on deck.

"Are you the one who brought this trouble on us?" asked one.

Jonah trembled, but then he nodded. He told his story:

Only days earlier, the Lord God of Heaven had commanded him to go to the city of Nineveh and tell its people to change their sinful ways. If they didn't, God would destroy them. But Jonah did not want to go to that evil city; the people of Nineveh had always been enemies of the people of Israel. Why should he do anything to help them? He tried to hide from God by going far away to Spain on this ship. But God had found him.

And so, the Lord had sent the storm that put the ship in peril. "Throw me overboard," he said. "Then God will calm the sea."

The sailors were horrified at the idea, but the storm only got worse. Finally, they decided they had no choice.

They grabbed Jonah by his shoulders and his feet. "Forgive us, Lord," they said. And they threw him over the side.

Instantly, the wind stopped and the waters began to calm. The sailors were amazed. Now they understood the power of Jonah's God.

God Saves Jonah

Jonah began to sink into the churning water. But as he sank, he prayed to God to save him.

God heard Jonah's prayers. He sent a huge fish rushing toward the drowning prophet. The fish opened its mouth and swallowed Jonah in one gulp. It was pitch black inside the fish, and Jonah was covered in slime and seaweed and chewed-up fish. The smell was unbearable, but he was alive.

Again he prayed:

"O God, when I was drowning, you rescued me. So even though I'm inside this fish, I praise you. And if you save me now, I will keep my promise and do what you asked of me."

Jonah stayed inside that fish for three days and three nights. Finally, God commanded the fish to vomit Jonah onto a nearby beach. Then God spoke to Jonah again.

"Now, go to the great city of Nineveh and tell the people to repent of their sins," God said. Jonah had learned his lesson, and he followed God's command. He began walking. Three days later, he arrived at the great city of Nineveh.

Jonah's Anger

Jonah preached to the people of Nineveh.

"God has found this city to be wicked and full of people doing evil. So forty days from now, Nineveh will be destroyed!"

The people were startled. "What does this mean?" they asked each other. "What can we do?"

"Repent before the Lord God Almighty," Jonah said. "Ask him to forgive your sins."

Before long, the king of Nineveh found out what Jonah was preaching. The king believed the word of God. He took off his expensive clothing and put on sackcloth. Then he issued an order:

"No one in Nineveh may eat or drink anything—even your animals must fast. You must wear sackcloth and pray to God with all your heart. Perhaps then God will change his mind and have mercy on us so that we won't be destroyed."

The people of Nineveh obeyed their king. And when God heard the people's prayers, he forgave all the evil they had done. God did not destroy their city.

Jonah was angry that God had decided not to destroy the Ninevites. He prayed again, but this prayer was very different than the others.

"Just let me die. When I was still in my own land, I knew you were a kind and merciful God. So why did you force me to come to this hateful country, if you were going to forgive the Ninevites?"

"What right do you have to be angry?" God asked.

But Jonah didn't understand. He was still mad. He walked out of the city and sat on a hill overlooking Nineveh, to see if God would change his mind. God caused a huge vine to grow over him to give him shade.

But the next morning, God sent a worm to chew on the vine and it withered, so Jonah had no shade. As the sun beat down on him, he again complained to God. "It is better for me to die than to live."

God then told Jonah something that made him think. "You feel badly about the vine which you did not create and labor over. So shouldn't I, your Lord God, have pity on my children, the Ninevites?"

Now Jonah knew that God looked after everyone, not just the people of Israel.

Think about it...

When Jonah disobeyed God and ran away, what do you think he learned? How would you behave if you were told to do something you didn't want to do?

All About Jonah and the Fish

DID YOU KNOW?

A Whale of a Fish

Many people call this story "Jonah and the Whale," but the Bible says it was a fish, not a whale, that saved Jonah. What kind of fish could swallow a man? It might have been a whale shark. These giants can be 30 feet long (almost as long as a 65-passenger school bus) and weigh 10 tons. It is not known to be a man-eater, but several dozen humans could fit in its belly.

whale shark

A Whale of a Tale

In the 1890's, James Bartley, a sailor on a whaling ship, went missing. His crewmates thought he must have fallen overboard. The crew caught an 80-foot long sperm whale and brought it home. When they cut it open, did they get a surprise! There was James Bartley inside the whale's stomach! His face, neck, and hands were bleached white, but he was alive. Like Jonah, he had survived for days inside the belly of a sea monster.

What's so great about Nineveh?

- Nineveh was in a part of the Middle East known then as the Assyrian Empire. It is now the country of Iraq.
- The city wall had 15 massive gates. Several of them have been reconstructed today.
- It had a library with thousands of clay tablets.
- It had a system of 18 canals which brought water to Nineveh.
- The palace built by King Sennacherib had 27 entrances and at least 80 chambers, halls, and rooms.
- At the time of Jonah, some 150,000 people lived there, making it one of the largest settlements in the world.

Sackcloth is a dark colored material made from goat or camel hair. This hair is very rough and scratchy.

Made in the Shade

The Book of Jonah was originally written in Hebrew. The Hebrew word for the vine that protected Jonah from the sun is *kikayon*, which means a plant with wide leaves. No one knows exactly what kind of plant it was. Some experts think it might have been a kind of gourd, such as the calabash, also called long melon, one of the first cultivated plants in the world. Others say it could have been a castor bean plant, which has large green leaves, is fast-growing, and can reach the size of a small tree, about 39 feet.

In all of the Bible, the word *kikayon* appears only in the Book of Jonah.

Daniel in the Lions' Den

Daniel 1–6

Daniel is rewarded for his faith in God.

Three men stood in front of Darius, king of Babylonia. They were the king's top aides. Each of them was the governor of a large part of the country.

From the look on the king's face, he was not happy.

"I am disappointed in the work you have been doing," he said. Then he looked directly at the oldest of the three men. "Except for you, Daniel. You take care of all the problems that arise in your sector. You keep good records. You are wise and honest."

Daniel bowed his head. "I serve the king as best I can," he said.

The king stood up. "And I thank you for it. Now I want to ask you to do even more. I want you to be my top aide. You will rule over all the governors and officials in my kingdom. Anyone who wants to talk to me must talk to you first. I know I can count on you to make sure that all the people of Babylonia obey the laws as you always do."

Again, Daniel bowed his head. "The king does me great honor," he said.

As the men left the throne room, the two other governors walked away together, looking back at Daniel with hate in their eyes.

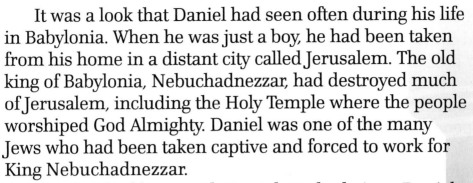

It was a look that Daniel had seen often during his life in Babylonia. When he was just a boy, he had been taken from his home in a distant city called Jerusalem. The old king of Babylonia, Nebuchadnezzar, had destroyed much of Jerusalem, including the Holy Temple where the people worshiped God Almighty. Daniel was one of the many Jews who had been taken captive and forced to work for King Nebuchadnezzar.

But God had been with Daniel. He had given Daniel the power to tell the meaning of dreams. Long ago, this gift had earned the praise of King Nebuchadnezzar. Ever since then, Daniel had been an important person in the king's palace.

Every day, Daniel passed places where the people who lived in the city of Babylon worshiped — glorious buildings with golden images of all their gods. He saw them doing things that made him look away in shame. He saw them eat food that was unclean to him. This was not the way of his people. But the kings of the country had always allowed him to worship God in the way he was taught. He was grateful for that, and satisfied with his life.

When Daniel arrived at his home, he placed his prayer shawl across his shoulders, and then stood by the window to pray to God as he did every day.

Two men were outside, watching him. These were the two governors who were now under Daniel.

"Daniel is getting too much power!" one said. "He doesn't even belong here — he's a foreigner. Why should he rule over you and me?"

The other man agreed. "If only we could think of a way to make the king turn against him."

"I know!" the first man cried. "I know what we can do. Hurry, let's go see the king again. I'll tell you my plan on the way."

Two days later, the king sent out a proclamation:

> *For the next thirty days, it is against the law for the people of Babylon to worship any god or man other than the king. Anyone who disobeys will be thrown into a pit of lions.*

Daniel's two enemies smiled when they heard about the proclamation. This had been their plan. They knew that the king was a very proud man who liked people to honor him. It had been easy to talk him into signing the new law.

That evening, the two men barged into Daniel's house when he was praying and grabbed him by the arms. "You're breaking the king's new law!" the first man cried.

Daniel had not heard about the law, but it didn't make any difference.

"No law is higher than God's law," he said.

"We'll see about that," said the second man. And they dragged Daniel off to the palace.

"This man broke your law," they told King Darius. "He must be punished. Throw him into the lion's den."

When King Darius heard what had happened, his face grew red with anger. He knew he had been tricked by the jealous men. But he had signed the new law and could not take it back. In Babylonia, no written law could be changed.

Sadly, he called his guards and they led Daniel to a deep pit in the ground. Three hungry lions paced back and forth on the floor of the pit.

"I am truly sorry, Daniel," the king said. "There is nothing I can do to stop this. May your God protect you from the lions."

The guards then grabbed Daniel and pushed him down into the hole. Then they picked up a big stone and placed it over the pit.

All night long, Darius tossed and turned in bed. He prayed to the God of Daniel that Daniel would be spared.

Early the next morning, he rushed to the pit.

"Daniel, are you still alive?"

A voice came from below. "I am, Great King."

Relieved, Darius ordered his men to move the stone that covered the pit. Down below, he saw Daniel standing quietly with the lions at his feet. They had not killed Daniel nor harmed him in any way.

The king breathed a sigh of relief. "How is it that you are still alive?" he asked.

Daniel replied, "My God knew I was innocent. He sent an angel to keep the lions from harming me."

The king ordered his men to lift Daniel out of the pit.

"I command everyone in my kingdom to worship and honor the God of Daniel. His God is the living God, the one who lives forever. And he rescues people and sets them free by working great miracles."

Think about it...

Daniel had to live among people who had different beliefs and customs than his own. How difficult do you think it would be to do that? How should we treat people who are trying to do the same in our country?

All About Daniel in the Lions' Den

The message on the wall was written in Hebrew. This is what Hebrew writing looks like.

The Handwriting on the Wall

Daniel was also a great prophet and interpreter of dreams. During the reign of King Belshazzar of Babylon, the king held a wild feast. During the feast, he held up holy objects that had been stolen from Solomon's Temple in Jerusalem and used them to praise the gods of gold and silver. Immediately, a ghostly hand appeared and wrote words on the wall of the royal palace. Daniel was brought in to interpret the omen. He told King Belshazzar that his kingdom would soon fall. That very night, King Belshazzar was killed. Today, the phrase "the handwriting is on the wall" is used to mean that great misfortune is on the way.

Ferocious Facts

- Lions that lived around Babylonia were known to eat cattle, sheep, and people too!
- The lion was the symbol of the Babylonian goddess of war, Ishtar.
- Sometimes, people hunted lions, trapped them in nets, but didn't kill them. They put them in cages so they could watch them for entertainment.

Don't Break the Law!

Throwing someone to the lions was just one of the strange ways the Babylonians punished people who broke the law. The punishment depended on how bad the crime was. Some people only had to pay a fine. If you did something serious, you could have your arms or legs chopped off. The Babylonians also forced many prisoners into slavery, or threw them into fiery pits.

Wonderful!

The Hanging Gardens of Babylon were said to be so amazing that they were known as one of the seven wonders of the ancient world. The seven wonders also included the Great Pyramid of Giza, the Temple of Artemis, the statue of Zeus at Olympia, the Colossus of Rhodes, the Mausoleum of Halicarnassus, and the Lighthouse of Alexandria. Of all of these, only the Great Pyramid remains today.

DID YOU KNOW?

In this story, Daniel puts a shawl around his shoulders when he prays. Many Jewish men of the time wore these prayer shawls, called tallits, whenever they worshiped. Some Jewish men today still follow this custom.

Where Was Babylonia?

Babylonia was an area in what is today Iraq and Syria. It was between two rivers, the Tigris and Euphrates. It was a beautiful country. The cities were large and airy, with many grand buildings that honored the gods which the Babylonians worshiped. Babylonians were wonderful artists, sculptors, and glassmakers. They were also very good farmers. They grew dates, wheat, barley, and other crops.

Fire from Heaven

1 Kings 18

How can Elijah prove that the God of Israel is the one true God?
Find out when you read this story.

It hadn't rained in the city of Samaria for three long years. The land was completely dry. It was getting harder and harder for the people to find food—even for Ahab, the king of Israel, who lived in Samaria.

"It's that prophet Elijah's fault," the king fumed. He remembered clearly the day when Elijah came to him and said, "As surely as the Lord God of Israel lives—the God whom I worship and serve—there will be no rain unless I give the word."

Now Elijah stood before him again, and King Ahab was angry.

"So here's Israel's troublemaker," the king said.

"I have made no trouble for Israel," Elijah replied. "It's you! It's you and your family who are the troublemakers because you have refused to worship the one true God. Instead, you have worshiped false gods, like Baal. And you have tempted all the people to worship false gods. Well, it's time you knew who is the true God of Israel."

So Elijah told King Ahab to bring all the people of Israel and the 850 prophets who served the king's gods to Mount Carmel.

As the people of Israel gathered, Elijah scolded them, "How long will it take you to make up your minds between

King Ahab's gods and the God of Israel? If the Lord is God, follow him! But if Baal is God, then follow him."

But the people remained silent. They refused to answer Elijah.

"It appears that I am the only prophet of the Lord left, so here's what we will do," Elijah said. "The prophets of Baal and I will have a contest. We'll each build an altar of wood and ask our god to light it. The god who answers and lights the fire will be the one true God."

King Ahab, the prophets, and the people all agreed.

Elijah let the prophets of Baal go first, since there were many more of them.

So the prophets of Baal got to work, piling the altar with wood for the fire.

All morning long, the prophets of Baal shouted to their god, "O Baal, answer us!" When no answer came, they shouted even louder and began to dance wildly around the altar.

"What's the matter with your god?" Elijah began to mock them. "Maybe you should pray louder. Or maybe Baal is day-dreaming, or off on a trip. Or maybe he's asleep."

149

This made the prophets of Baal mad, so they shouted even louder. They ranted and raved all afternoon into the evening. But there was no reply. No voice answered. No fire appeared.

Then Elijah called to the people, "Come over here. Help me repair the Lord's altar that's been torn down by the king."

So the people helped rebuild the altar, using twelve stones to represent the twelve tribes of Israel. Then Elijah placed the wood on the altar and dug a ditch around it.

Next he told the people, "Fill four large jars of water and pour it all over the altar." After the people had emptied their water jars, Elijah said, "Now do it again."

When they were finished, Elijah told them to pour water over the altar a third time. There was so much water that it filled the ditch.

"This is crazy," one man said to another. "Not even the true God could make this wood burn. It's soaked through!"

Elijah walked up to the altar, looked up to heaven, and prayed, "O Lord, prove today that you are the God of Israel and that I am your servant. O Lord, answer me so that the people will know that you are God and that you have brought them back to you."

Immediately, a huge flash of fire came down from heaven! It burned up the altar, the wood, and the stones. The flames even burned up all the water in the ditch!

When the people saw this, they fell on their faces and cried out, "The Lord is God! The Lord is God!"

Then Elijah told King Ahab to go home. "Go and enjoy a good meal! For the people now know the truth, and I hear a mighty rainstorm coming."

Sure enough, the sky became black with clouds. A strong wind brought in a terrific rainstorm. The drought had ended and everyone knew who was the one true God.

Think about it...

When have you stood against a group of friends because you didn't agree with what they were doing? How did you feel? What helped you stick to what you believed?

All About Fire From Heaven

Divided Nation

After King Solomon died, there was disagreement about who would be the next king. Solomon's son, Rehoboam, was supposed to rule over all twelve tribes of Israel. Instead, one of King Solomon's officials rebelled and took ten of those tribes away from Rehoboam. From that moment on, Israel was two nations. The northern part, with ten tribes, kept the name Israel. The southern part, with two tribes, was named Judah.

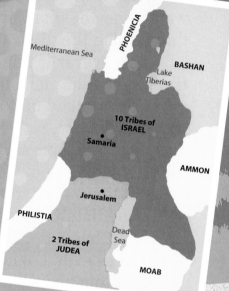

Mediterranean Sea

PHOENICIA

BASHAN

Lake Tiberias

10 Tribes of ISRAEL

Samaria

AMMON

Jerusalem

PHILISTIA

Dead Sea

2 Tribes of JUDEA

MOAB

DID YOU KNOW?

Elijah was taken to heaven in a whirlwind, riding in a chariot that was all aflame.

Mean King Ahab

Ahab was the seventh king of the new Israel. He did not obey God's law; he was cruel and ruthless, and worshiped false gods. Over the centuries, the name Ahab came to mean "a man who is evil." In the classic tale *Moby Dick*, writer Herman Melville named the captain of a whaling ship after the biblical king. Melville's Ahab was just as mean as his namesake.

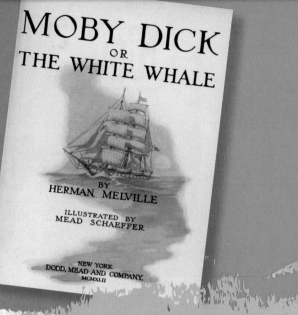

MOBY DICK
OR
THE WHITE WHALE

BY
HERMAN MELVILLE

ILLUSTRATED BY
MEAD SCHAEFFER

NEW YORK
DODD, MEAD AND COMPANY.
MCMXLII

WHAT IS A PROPHET?

A prophet is a person who speaks the word of God. God gave some prophets the power to do miracles. Some of God's prophets include:

- Elisha, who followed Elijah. Elisha performed many miracles, including parting the Jordan River and feeding 100 men from only 20 loaves of barley.
- Isaiah, who told of events that would—and did—happen in Israel hundreds of years later.
- Daniel, who survived a night in the lions' den, but also preached that God was all knowing and would defeat evil and deliver those who are faithful.

Who was Baal?

Baal was the name the people of Canaan gave to the god of rain. Baal's name means "lord" or "master." Baal was so important that many Canaanites considered him a super god, the king of all the gods. The Canaanites believed Baal provided everything that they needed to survive, including herds of livestock and their farms.

The Invisible Guest

At every Passover Seder, a place is set for Elijah as a symbol of hope that he will return one day. Some families like to play a game with their children. At some time during the dinner, the children are sent to the door to let Elijah in. If an adult has been quick enough, the children return to find that some of the wine in Elijah's cup has been drunk—"proof" that Elijah had come in.

The Birth of Jesus

Matthew 1.18–25; 2.1–12; Luke 2.1–20

The people of Israel had lost faith in God. They needed a savior who would show them the power of God and his love for them. That special person was born in a stable, in the town of Bethlehem.

Joseph hoisted another large timber onto his carpenter's bench. Wiping his forehead, he headed for the water jar to get a drink. As Joseph dipped his cup into the water, a beautiful young girl walked into the courtyard.

Joseph greeted the girl, who was soon to be his wife.

"Mary, I didn't expect to see you today."

"I must speak with you," Mary said.

"You seem troubled," Joseph said. "Has something happened?"

Mary took a deep breath and said, "An angel appeared to me today."

Joseph's mouth dropped open. "What?"

"It really was an angel," Mary said in a soft voice, as if she still couldn't believe it. "I was scared at first, but the angel told me not to be afraid. He said that I have been chosen to be the mother of God's Promised Son. I am already with child."

Joseph stared at her. "But, Mary, what will people say? We aren't married yet."

"I only know what the angel has told me—that I am to have a baby by God's Holy Spirit."

Joseph was a good man, but this news troubled him.

He didn't want to embarrass Mary, but he thought it might be best to call off the wedding. That night, Joseph tossed and turned for hours, trying to decide what to do. At long last, he fell into a fitful sleep and had a dream. In his dream, an angel spoke to him.

"Joseph, don't be afraid to make Mary your wife," the angel said. "What she said is true. Her baby is God's Son. You must name him Jesus."

When Joseph awoke, he was no longer upset. He married Mary right away.

A Long Journey

Mary and Joseph lived in the city of Nazareth. One day, a messenger from Rome came to Nazareth with an announcement.

"Our great emperor, Caesar Augustus, has commanded that everyone will pay taxes to Rome. Each person must return to the city where his family came from to be counted! There will be no exceptions."

Joseph was from the family of King David, so he and Mary would have to travel to the city of David, which was Bethlehem.

Mary was upset. "Bethlehem? Oh, Joseph! That's a long journey. The baby... he's about to be born!"

Joseph put his arms around her and said, "We have no choice."

The Miracle in the Stable

Bethlehem was crowded with people when they arrived. Joseph tried to find a room where Mary could rest.

"I'm sorry," the innkeeper said. "We're full." But when he saw that Mary was with child, he took pity. "I suppose you could stay in the stable," he said. "It's warm, and there's plenty of clean hay to sleep on."

Joseph thanked him and led Mary to the stable.

A few donkeys, some goats and sheep, and even an ox, looked at them curiously. Mice scurried underfoot.

Joseph helped Mary lie down on the hay, and he spread his cloak over her to protect her from the cold.

Sometime during that night, Mary's baby was born.

Joseph picked up the squalling infant, wrapped him in swaddling clothes, and then tucked him close to Mary. She held the child in her arms whispering comforting words to him. When he fell asleep, she put him in a manger filled with straw. As the angel had commanded, they named the baby, Jesus.

The First Worshipers

In fields nearby, shepherds huddled around their campfire trying to keep warm. It was, they thought, a very ordinary night. The sheep were quiet, the stars so close they could almost pick them out of the sky. Then there was a burst of light, and an angel appeared before them. The shepherds were terrified!

"Don't be afraid," the angel said. "I have great news that will bring joy to people everywhere. Today in Bethlehem a child was born—a Savior, Christ the Lord. You will find him lying in a manger in a stable."

Instantly, the sky filled up with angels singing. Then they vanished as quickly as they had appeared.

The stunned shepherds left their flocks and went in search of the baby. They found Joseph, Mary, and baby Jesus in the stable with the animals gathered around them.

The shepherds told Mary and Joseph about the angels and their news. Mary's heart was filled with joy when she realized that God had spoken to these humble men and told them what she already knew. Her baby was God's only Son—the Savior the people had been waiting for.

The shepherds were not the baby's only visitors. Months earlier and far away to the east, some wise men had seen an especially bright star in the sky. These men believed the star would lead them to a new king born somewhere in Israel. So they set out to find him.

The men had followed the star for weeks and weeks—all the way to Bethlehem. By this time, Mary and Joseph had found a house to stay in. It was there that the wise men found the baby who would grow up to be the King of Kings.

"We have brought gifts for the King," they said, placing before the baby objects of gold and jars of precious myrrh and frankincense.

Then they knelt down and worshiped him in awe and wonder.

Think about it...

One of the names for Jesus is Immanuel. Immanuel means "God is with us." What does it mean to you that God is with us?

All About the Birth of Jesus

Who were the Wise Men?

The story in the Bible does not give the names of the wise men; it says only that "some wise men" came from the East. The wise men, or magi, may have been astrologers who believed that when a great leader was born, a new star would appear in the sky. Because they brought three gifts, it is believed that there were three of them. Later Christian writers called them kings, and gave them the names Balthazar, Melchior, and Gaspar.

In those days, some astronomers used an instrument called an astrolabe to track the movement of the stars.

DID YOU KNOW?

A manger is a trough or box made of carved stone or wood used to hold food for animals in a stable.

Star of Wonder

Scientists still wonder about the Star of Bethlehem, also known as the Christmas Star, that led the magi to Jesus' birthplace. Was it a single exploding star? A comet? Some believe the "star" could have been two planets, Venus and Jupiter, which had been observed moving closer together in the years 3 B.C. and 2 B.C. The planets' movements certainly would have caught the attention of ancient astrologers—like the magi.

THREE GIFTS

Frankincense and myrrh (sounds like *mrrr*) are both sweet-smelling powders made from plants that grow in desert-like places. They were very expensive and almost as precious as gold.

BABY WRAP

Newborn babies were wrapped up tightly (swaddled) in a piece of soft cloth so that they could not wave their arms and legs about. This was to keep the baby still and warm.

SO HOW FAR IS BETHLEHEM?

The distance from Nazareth to Bethlehem is 70 miles as the crow flies. On the direct route that Joseph and Mary probably took, the journey could have been done in three or four days, or it might have taken a week. In any case, it was a major undertaking for anyone about to have a baby!

Living Nativity

At Christmas, churches around the world recreate the scene of Jesus' birth (called the Nativity) using actors and live animals. This tradition was started in the 13th century by Saint Francis of Assisi, a Catholic friar and teacher who lived in Italy.

John and Jesus

Matthew 3.1–17; Mark 1.1–12; Luke 3.1–22

Jesus is baptized, then blessed by God, his Father.

John was standing in the Jordan River, ready to baptize all who were truly sorry they had disobeyed God's commandments.

John was a strong, lean man who lived in the desert. He did not need money or jewelry and fancy clothes. He wore clothes made of camel's hair held around his waist with a leather strap. For his dinner, he was happy with a meal of grasshoppers and honey.

John cared only about pleasing God. God had brought him into the world for a special purpose: to prepare the people of Israel for the coming of a Savior. This Savior had been born in Bethlehem almost thirty years before John began to preach.

Now people were streaming to the place where John preached. They came from Jerusalem and Judea and the Jordan River Valley.

John told them, "Be kind to the poor. If you have two coats, give one to someone who doesn't have any. If you have food, share it with someone else."

They wondered, *Could John be the Messiah, the one the prophets said would come to save us?*

But John said, "Someone more powerful is going to come. I am not good enough to untie his sandals. I am just baptizing with water. He will baptize you with the Holy Spirit."

John was talking about Jesus, who lived in the town of Nazareth. The baby who had been born in a stable in Bethlehem was now a grown man. He had been working as a carpenter with his father, Joseph, since he was a child.

One morning, Jesus woke up and felt that his life was about to change. He had always known that God had a plan for him. It was now time to begin.

Jesus left Nazareth and walked to the Jordan River.

"I have come to be baptized," he told John.

John knew who Jesus was. "No, no," he said. "I am the one who should be baptized by you."

But Jesus said, "For now this is how it should be. We must do all that God wants us to do."

And so John baptized Jesus. As soon as Jesus came out of the water, the sky opened and the Spirit of God came down on him like a dove. A voice from heaven said, "This is my dear Son, and I am pleased with him."

Think about it...

How did John know which people to baptize? Why do you think he wanted Jesus to baptize him?

All About
John and Jesus

What Happened to John the Baptist?

John got in trouble with King Herod, who ruled over Galilee. The king had broken the law of Moses by getting married to his brother's wife while the brother was still alive. John spoke out against him. This made the king so angry that he had John put into prison. Later, the king ordered a guard to execute John by cutting off his head. John's followers buried him and told Jesus what had happened.

DID YOU KNOW?

John and Jesus were cousins. Elizabeth, the mother of John the Baptist, was related to Mary, the mother of Jesus.

RESPECT

At the time of Jesus it was the job of slaves or servants to tie the master's sandals. When John said he was not good enough to tie Jesus' sandals, he meant that, compared to Jesus, he was just a simple, common man.

Down by the river

John baptized people on both the east side and west side of the Jordan River. This site on the east side in the country of Jordan is believed to be the place where John baptized Jesus. It was discovered in the 1990s, when scientists dug up buried ruins that dated back to the time of Jesus.

The Crippled Man
Matthew 9.1–8; Mark 2.1–12; Luke 5.17–26

When Jesus began teaching God's word, God gave him the power to heal people who were sick, crippled, or blind. Wherever he went, large crowds came to hear him preach and to be cured of their diseases.

The small fishing village of Capernaum was abuzz—Jesus was coming!

A man passing through the town heard the talk and rushed home to find his friends. He was thinking about one of their neighbors, a man who was crippled and could not walk.

"Have you heard about this Jesus?" the man asked. "The people say that he performs miracles and can heal any disease or sickness. Maybe we should take our neighbor to see him."

The friends agreed, and the four of them placed their neighbor on a mat. They carried him over to the house where Jesus was preaching. When they got there, people were spilling out of the door.

One of the friends said to the crippled man, "I'm sorry, we can't get through this crowd."

The man was disappointed, but he said, "You tried, my friends. Just take me back home."

But the oldest man said, "Wait, I have an idea. Come with me."

The men carried the mat to the side of the house where stairs led up to the roof. The oldest man stepped onto the first stair.

"Careful now," he said. Together, the four strong men lifted the mat and climbed the stairs.

The crippled man was alarmed. "What are you doing?" he asked.

"You'll see," his friend said. "Don't worry. We won't drop you."

When they got to the top, the men set the mat down on the flat roof, which was made from layers of branches that were packed together with dried mud. Then they got down on their hands and knees and began to pull up the branches to make an opening a little larger than the mat.

Slowly and carefully, they lowered their friend through the hole in the roof until the mat came to rest on the floor right in front of Jesus!

The crowd couldn't believe the boldness of these men, but Jesus was pleased by their faith. He looked down at the crippled man and said, "My friend, your sins are forgiven."

The religious leaders in the crowd gasped and muttered to each other, "Who does he think he is? Only God can forgive sins!"

Jesus looked at the leaders and asked, "Why do you say such things? Tell me, which do you think is easier—to tell this man that his sins are forgiven, or to tell him to get up and walk? I will show you that I have the right to forgive sins."

Turning to the crippled man, Jesus said, "Stand up, take your mat and go home because you are healed."

As the people watched in wonder, the man got to his feet. He picked up his mat and pushed his way through the stunned crowd. The crowd began to praise God, saying, "We have never seen anything like this before!"

The Roman Officer
Matthew 8.5–13; Luke 7.1–10

One day, Jesus was preaching to a group of people on the main street of Capernaum. The crowd moved away when a Roman officer walked up to

Jesus. He was one of the centurions—officers who were in charge of one hundred soldiers.

The soldiers had been sent by the Emperor of Rome to keep order in Capernaum.

Now, the Jewish people didn't like being ruled by the emperor, and they didn't trust the Roman soldiers. But Jesus greeted the centurion like any other man.

Quietly, the centurion spoke to Jesus. "Lord, my young servant is in such terrible pain that he can't get out of bed. He can't even move."

Jesus answered him, "I will come and heal him."

"No, my Lord!" the centurion replied. "Lord, I'm not good enough for you to come into my house. I know you can make it happen right now with just one word. I know because I am in charge of my soldiers. All I have to do is give an order, and they do it."

Jesus looked at the centurion in amazement. Then he spoke to the crowd, "Did you hear this Roman?" he said. "I have not seen faith like his in all of Israel!"

Jesus turned back to the centurion. "Go home. Your faith has made it happen."

When the centurion returned home, he discovered his servant completely recovered and doing his regular chores. In fact, the young man had been healed at the exact moment that Jesus had said the words!

Blind Bartimaeus
Matthew 20.29–34; Mark 10.46–52; Luke 18.35–43

Jesus and his disciples were on their way to Jerusalem and had stopped for a while in the city of Jericho. They didn't stay long, but as they were leaving a huge crowd of people followed them. A blind beggar named Bartimaeus was sitting in his usual spot by the side of the road when he heard the commotion.

"What's going on?" he asked. "Someone, please tell me what's happening?"

"Quiet, you," said a man. "Jesus is coming down the road with his followers."

Jesus? Bartimaeus couldn't see, but he had certainly heard the stories about Jesus and the miracles he had performed—especially how he could heal any kind of sickness or infirmity. Could it be possible that Jesus was going to pass right by him? Maybe Jesus could heal him!

Filled with hope, Bartimaeus began shouting, "Jesus, Son of David, have pity on me!"

Some in the crowd turned to Bartimaeus in disgust and said, "Be quiet! Don't bother him. You're only a beggar—why would Jesus want to help you?"

But Bartimaeus yelled even louder, "Son of David, have pity on me!"

Jesus stopped. He turned toward Bartimaeus. "Tell that man to come here."

Someone in the crowd called to Bartimaeus, "Take heart! Jesus heard you. He wants you to go to him."

At that, Bartimaeus jumped up, letting his coat fall to the ground. The people led him to Jesus.

Jesus asked him, "What do you want me to do for you?"

"Teacher, I have been blind for as long as I can remember. I want to see," Bartimaeus answered.

And Jesus said to him, "Go on your way. Your eyes are healed because of your faith."

At that very instant, Bartimaeus could see! He followed Jesus down the road, praising God for healing him. And those who witnessed this miracle praised God as well.

The Ten Lepers
Luke 17.11–19

Everywhere Jesus went, people recognized him. As soon as they heard he was coming, residents of the villages, the neighboring towns, and even the farms, would bring their sick friends and relatives so that Jesus might see and heal them.

One day, Jesus was on his way to Jerusalem with his disciples. They entered a village near Samaria. A group of men stood far apart from everyone else in the village. Jesus knew the men must have the horrible skin disease known as leprosy. People with this disease were given the name, leper. It was believed that anyone who got close to a leper would get the disease. So, no one could go near them and they could not go near anyone, not even their own families.

When the ten men saw Jesus, they called out, "Jesus, Master, please help us."

Jesus looked at them and told them, "You are healed. Go show yourselves to the priests."

The lepers could see the sores on their arms and feet disappearing. But before they could go home, they had to show the priests that they had been healed. The men ran off.

One man had not gone far when he stopped. The others kept going, but this one turned around and ran back to Jesus, shouting, "Praise God! Praise God! I am healed!"

When he reached Jesus, the man fell down on his face before Jesus.

"Thank you, Master. Thank you, Jesus, for healing me," the man said over and over.

Jesus reached out to the man. "You are a Samaritan, aren't you?" The man nodded, afraid that Jesus would turn away from him. Jewish people in Judea usually didn't have anything to do with Samaritans, who had different beliefs and never welcomed other Jews to their villages.

"Didn't I heal ten lepers?" Jesus asked his followers. "Where are the other nine? Is this foreigner the only one to come back and give thanks to God?"

And Jesus said to the man, "Stand up, friend. It is your faith that has made you well."

The man continued to praise God and told everyone who had healed him!

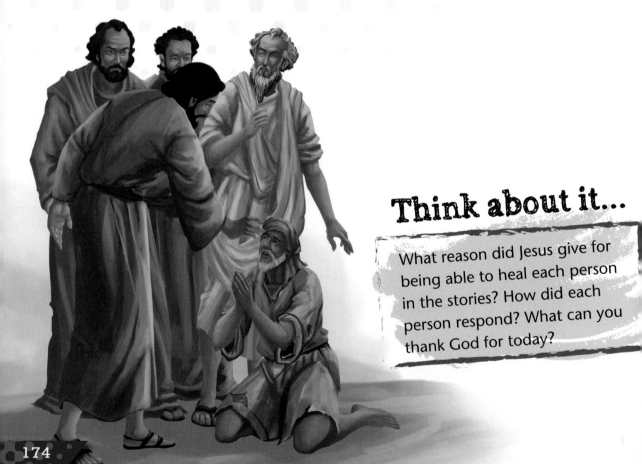

Think about it...

What reason did Jesus give for being able to heal each person in the stories? How did each person respond? What can you thank God for today?

All About
Jesus the Healer

Up on the Roof

How many rooms does your house have? Most houses in the time of Jesus had just one room where the family ate and slept, and sometimes kept animals, too! The flat roofs were like a second floor. On the roof, they could grow vegetables, wash and dry clothes, and take baths. Best of all, the roof was a good place to sleep on a hot night.

WHAT IS LEPROSY?

Known today as Hansen's disease, leprosy is an infectious disease that produces horrible sores and numbness in the arms and legs. At one time, people believed that leprosy caused a person's fingers, nose, or other body parts to fall off. People get leprosy by inhaling a certain bacteria. Although leprosy was common in biblical times, only 100 cases are diagnosed each year in the United States. Doctors can treat leprosy with drugs.

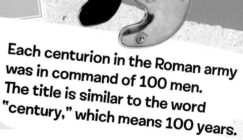

Each centurion in the Roman army was in command of 100 men. The title is similar to the word "century," which means 100 years.

Why did people call Jesus the "Son of David?"

King David was one of Jesus' ancestors. Those who believed Jesus was the Messiah referred to him as the Son of David because it was promised that the Messiah would come from King David's family.

DID YOU KNOW?

TWO Parables

Luke 10.25–37; 15.1–7, 11–32

Jesus knew that sometimes the best way to teach was with a story.

A group of people was gathered around Jesus. Some of them believed what Jesus was teaching, and some did not. One believer asked, "Teacher, what does God want me to do?"

"Love the Lord your God with all your heart, soul, and mind," Jesus told him. "And be kind to your neighbors. Treat them the way you want them to treat you."

"Very well and good," another man said. He was also a teacher, and he was sure he knew more about God than Jesus did. "But who are my neighbors?"

Jesus told him this story.

The Good Samaritan

A man was walking along the road from Jerusalem to Jericho. Suddenly, three robbers jumped out from behind a tree. They grabbed his bags and his money purse and beat him up. Then they ran off.

The man lay beside the road, half dead.

A short time later, a priest came along the same road. He saw the injured man. "Hmm," he said to himself. "That poor fellow looks half dead. But I can't do anything about it now."

So he crossed to the other side of the road and went on his way. Later, a worker at the temple came by. "Hmm," he said. "I don't have time to get involved." And he, too, walked across the road and continued on his journey.

Next, a man riding a donkey came along. He was from Samaria, a region north of Judea. The Samaritans were also Jews, but they were not welcome in Jerusalem. They had their own beliefs, and the people in Judea did not trust them. Nor did the Samaritans trust the Jews in Judea.

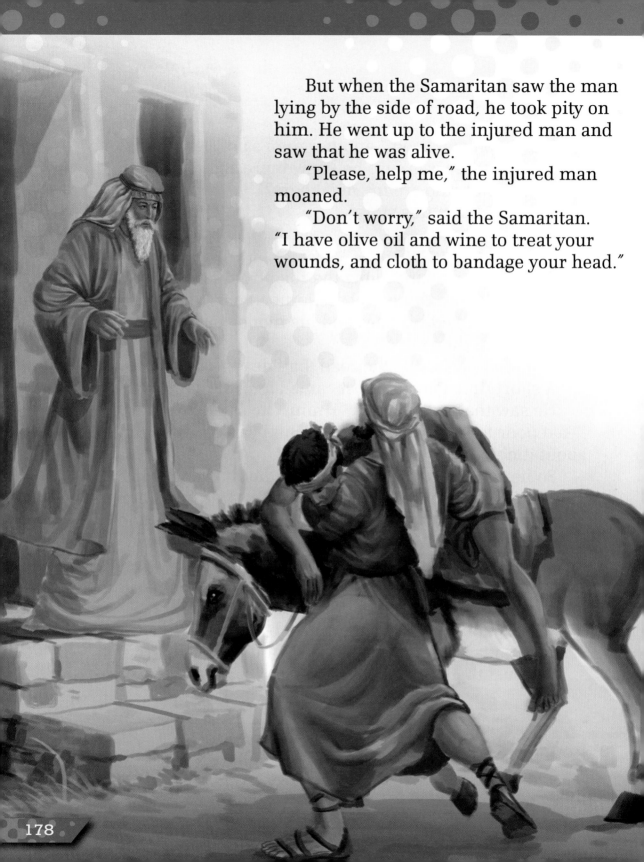

But when the Samaritan saw the man lying by the side of road, he took pity on him. He went up to the injured man and saw that he was alive.

"Please, help me," the injured man moaned.

"Don't worry," said the Samaritan. "I have olive oil and wine to treat your wounds, and cloth to bandage your head."

After he took care of the man's wounds, the Samaritan lifted him up and put him on his donkey. He led the donkey along the road until they came to an inn.

The Samaritan spent the night at the inn taking care of the injured man. The next morning, he went to the innkeeper.

"I must be on my way now," he said. "Please take care of the man." He handed the innkeeper two silver coins.

"If you spend more than this on him, I will pay you on my way back home."

Jesus stopped talking. Then he looked at the teacher and said, "Which of these three people was a real neighbor to the man who was beaten up?"

There was only one answer the teacher could give: "The one who showed pity."

Jesus said, "Go and do the same!"

• • •

Another day, Jesus welcomed a tax collector to the group that was listening to him. No one was more hated than the tax collector who cheated the people whenever he had the chance. Some of the religious leaders in the village thought that Jesus was wrong to make friends with tax collectors.

"Look at him!" one of the leaders said. "He teaches about God and the kingdom of heaven, but then he hangs out with all kinds of bad people!"

"I know," said another. "He even eats with them! What kind of teacher keeps company with such people?"

Jesus heard the men and invited them to join him.

"Do you want to know what God's love is really like?" he said. And he told them this story:

The Prodigal Son

A rich man had two sons. One day the younger son came to him and said, "Father, I want my share of your wealth now. I don't want to wait for it until you die."

The father was very sad to hear his son's request, but he agreed and divided his money between his two sons.

A few days later, the younger son packed up everything and left for a distant country, far from his father's home.

"Now I can do anything I please," he said to himself. And that's what he did. The young man went out every night. He went to wild parties. He spent all his money on fine clothes and the best things to eat. Soon, he had no money left.

About that time, a famine hit the land. There was nothing to eat. To keep from starving, the young man went to a local farm and begged the farmer to give him a job feeding the pigs. The farmer agreed, and the young man took the job. He was so hungry that he even ate the pigs' food.

One day, he woke up and said, "What am I doing? What am I thinking? Even my father's hired hands have more to eat than I do. I will go home and ask my father to forgive me. Maybe, just maybe, he'll hire me as a worker."

After walking for many days, the young man saw his father's house above the road at the top of a hill. He stopped. *What will my father say when he sees me?* he thought. *Will he turn me away?*

But just then he saw a man running down the hill. His father! When he reached his son, the father took him in his arms.

"I am so glad to see you! Welcome home, son," the father said, his eyes filled with tears of happiness.

The son quickly said, "Father, I am so sorry. I don't deserve your kindness. I have treated you badly. I have spent all the money you gave me on foolish things. I'm not worthy to be your son any more."

The father had already forgiven him. He took his son back to the house and ordered his servants to find the finest robe for him. Then he gave his son a beautiful ring and brand-new sandals.

"We must celebrate!" he told his servants. "Find the fattest calf and prepare a great feast. I thought I would never see my son again, but now he is here. I thought he was lost, but now he's found!"

As the father ordered his servants to prepare the feast, he noticed his older son sulking in the corner. "My boy," said the father. "What is wrong? Why do you look so angry? Come and join the celebration."

The older son shook his head and complained, "All these years I worked hard for you, but you never honored me with a feast. You never gave me a fine robe or a ring. Yet, my younger brother throws away your money on wild living—and you treat him like a hero!"

"Oh, my dear boy, my son," the father said tenderly. "You and I are very close. Everything I have is yours. There is nothing I would refuse you. But look, your brother was dead, now he is alive! Your brother was lost, but now he is found. We have to celebrate!"

. . .

Jesus stopped talking and the crowd was completely quiet. He looked straight at the religious leaders.

"God's love is just like that," he told them. "He rejoices whenever someone comes back to him."

Think about The Good Samaritan...

Based on this story, how do you think God wants us to treat other people? In what ways can you show God's love to others?

Think about The Prodigal Son...

What do you think about how the rich man treated his two sons? Did the older son have a right to be unhappy?

DID YOU KNOW?

A parable is a short story that teaches something important about life.

GOLDEN WORDS

When someone tells you to "follow the golden rule" they're simply referring to what Jesus said: treat others as you would want them to treat you.

Take Your Medicine

The Good Samaritan used oil mixed with wine to heal the injured man's wounds. Other medicines of this time included herbs, such as rosemary, used to cure stomach aches, and plants like maidenhair fern, to get rid of tapeworms. One of these old medicines is still used today: can you guess what it is? Honey, for sore throats!

What does the phrase "prodigal son" mean?

The word "prodigal" means wasteful and reckless. In this story, the wasteful and reckless son returned to the people who loved him. A person who behaves this way is often called a "prodigal son."

REAL-LIFE HEROES

Today, we use the words "Good Samaritan" to describe a person who goes out of his way to help someone without expecting a reward. Most states have Good Samaritan laws that prevent anyone from suing a Good Samaritan in court if the accident victim is injured while being helped.

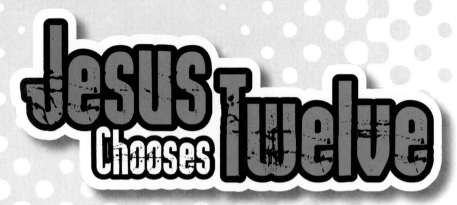

Jesus Chooses Twelve

Matthew 4.18–22; 10.1–4; Mark 1.16–20; 3.13–19; Luke 5.1–11; 6.12–16

Jesus chose men he could trust to help him bring the news about God's kingdom to the people. These men would be his special disciples. The first four were fishermen.

Lake Galilee was bathed in moonlight. It was a good night for fishing.

Simon and his brother, Andrew, pulled up their nets. Nothing. Not one fish.

"James! John!" Simon called to two brothers who were fishing nearby. "Did you catch anything?"

"Our nets are empty," James said. "We'll have to keep fishing until dawn. Maybe our luck will change."

But at dawn, the fishermen were on the shore of Lake Galilee washing their nets. Their boats were empty. They had nothing to show for their night's work.

Suddenly, the men heard voices. They looked up and saw a crowd of people walking toward the lake. One man stood apart from the others. Simon heard someone call the man, Jesus.

Jesus! This was the man from Nazareth who was in Capernaum preaching about God's kingdom.

Simon and Andrew could only stare in wonder as Jesus came right up to the shore. His followers were crowding around him so closely that he could barely move.

Jesus looked at Simon and said, "Take me out in your boat so that all these people will be able to hear me."

Simon rowed Jesus out a short way, and Jesus began speaking to the people on the shore. When he was finished teaching, he turned to Simon and Andrew.

"Go out into the deep water and let your nets down to catch some fish."

Simon was startled. "Master," he said, "there are no fish. We have been fishing all night long and have not caught anything."

But then Simon paused. After all, this was Jesus! "All right," he said. "If you tell me to, I will let the nets down." Simon took the boat farther from shore, and he and Andrew dropped their nets.

When they pulled up the first one, it was so full of fish that some of the strings broke! The same thing happened when they pulled up the second net.

Simon called to James and John. They rowed out and dropped their nets. They, too, caught so many fish that their boat started to sink.

"How can this be happening?" asked Simon. "How can there be hundreds of fish where there were none before?"

Jesus told Simon, "Don't be afraid. This is what God wants you to do. From now on, you will bring in people instead of fish. You will gather them to me so that they can hear the lessons that I teach."

So the fishermen pulled their boats to shore and gladly followed Jesus.

Soon after, Jesus went up to a mountain to pray. He stayed there all night. The next morning, his followers gathered to hear him.

"God has told me to choose twelve of you to come with me and help teach the people about the kingdom."

These are the men Jesus chose that day:

The four fishermen, Simon (Jesus named him Peter); Andrew; and James and John, the sons of Zebedee.

The others Jesus chose were Philip; Bartholomew; Thomas; Levi (who Jesus called Matthew); James, the son of Alphaeus; Thaddaeus; Simon; and Judas Iscariot.

The disciples went with Jesus all over Judea and Jerusalem and as far as the cities of Tyre and Sidon on the coast of the Mediterranean Sea.

Think about it...

The twelve disciples didn't think twice about following Jesus. What does this tell you about Jesus?

All About
Jesus' Disciples

Go Fish

Fish were a major part of the family's diet in ancient Israel, and fishermen had to work hard to keep up with the demand. Most fishing took place on Lake Galilee either from boats or from the shore. A single fisherman could catch a lot of fish with his large round net. He would spin the net over his head and throw (cast) it into the shallow water. Stones or other weights tied to the outside made the net sink. When fish swam over the net, the fisherman pulled a line. The net closed around the fish—and the fisherman brought dinner home to his family.

DID YOU KNOW?

"Disciple" is another word for "student." Many people who followed Jesus became his disciples.

What was special about the twelve disciples?

These disciples were chosen to follow Jesus, receive his teachings, and witness the miracles he performed. All, except Judas Iscariot, became apostles who taught Jesus' message and carried on his work.

Jesus Teaches on a Mountain

Matthew 4–7

People came from far and near to hear Jesus teach the word of God.

Two men from the city of Pella were walking along the road to Galilee.

"Do you think Jesus will welcome us?" one man asked his friend. "Or will he turn us away? After all, we are strangers here. We don't follow the Jewish laws of Galilee."

"I have heard that he welcomes everyone who wants to learn the word of God," his friend said. "He doesn't ask where you live. He doesn't care what you do for a living. Do you know that he cured a crippled man just by telling him to get up and walk? Truly, this man is like no one else on earth."

As they got closer to Galilee, they saw other travelers going in the same direction. Soon, more groups arrived. They all entered the town of Capernaum together. It was easy to find Jesus. He was sitting on a mountain with his twelve disciples around him. The men from Pella and all the others sat down with the others. They listened as Jesus began speaking about the blessings of God.

"God blesses those people who depend only on him.
They belong to the kingdom of heaven!
God blesses those people who grieve.
They will find comfort!

God blesses those people who are humble.
The earth will belong to them!
God blesses those people who make peace.
They will be called his children!
God blesses those people who are treated badly for
doing right.
They belong to the kingdom of heaven."
Jesus continued speaking about God's blessings.
His words swept over everyone who listened and
gave them peace.
Jesus had many other messages about the way God wanted
people to live their lives. He said, "You who listen to God are
like a light for the whole world, and a light must not
be hidden. No one would light a lamp
and put it under a clay pot.
Make your light shine so
that others will see the
good you do."
He said, "You have
been taught, 'An eye
for an eye and a tooth
for a tooth.' But I tell
you that it is wrong
to get even with
a person who has
done something bad
to you."
"When someone
slaps your right cheek,
turn and let the person
slap your other cheek."

The people listened with all their hearts and minds. The only sound was the cries of birds flying above faraway Lake Galilee.

Jesus told them: "You have heard people say, 'Love your neighbors and hate your enemies.' But I tell you to love your enemies and pray for anyone who treats you badly. Then you will be acting like your Father in heaven."

"When you do good deeds, don't try to show off. When you give to the poor, don't let anyone know. Your Father knows, and he will reward you."

"Ask, and you shall receive. Search, and you will find. Knock, and the door will be opened to you. Your heavenly Father is ready to give good things to people who ask."

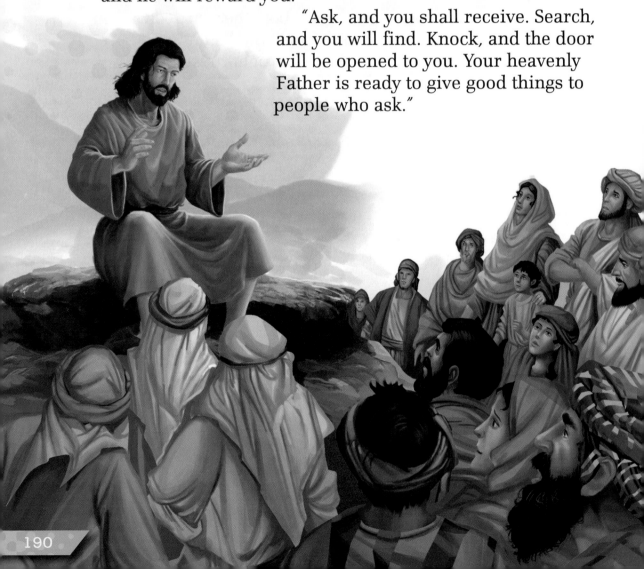

He warned the people to be careful about how they judge others.

"Watch out for false prophets! They dress up like sheep but inside they are wolves. You can tell what they are by what they do."

"Don't give a dog what belongs to God. It will only turn and attack you. Don't throw pearls down in front of pigs. They will trample all over them."

The light was fading in the sky as Jesus came to the end of his lessons.

"Anyone who hears and obeys my teachings is like a wise person who built a house on solid rock. Rains poured down, rivers flooded, and winds blew, but the house did not fall."

"Anyone who hears but does not obey my teachings is like a person who built a house on sand. The rain poured down, the rivers flooded, and the winds blew. Finally, the house fell with a crash."

The crowd broke up and the men from Pella began the journey back to their city.

"I have never heard a teacher like him," one man said.

Everyone agreed. They would take the words of Jesus to everyone in their town so that all the people would know how much God loves them.

Think about it...

Which of Jesus' teachings means the most to you? Which ones could you start following today?

What was different about Pella?

Pella was only about 40 miles from Galilee, but the people followed the customs of the country of Greece, which had once ruled Palestine. They believed that everything in life was ruled by gods and goddesses. They built temples to honor them. One temple in Pella honored Artemis, the goddess of hunting.

Where was the mountain on which Jesus taught?

Although the Bible does not give the name of the mountain on which Jesus taught, many people believe it was Mount Tabor, a large hill 11 miles west of the Sea of Galilee. However, others believe it was Karn Hattin, where the Church of the Beatitudes now sits.

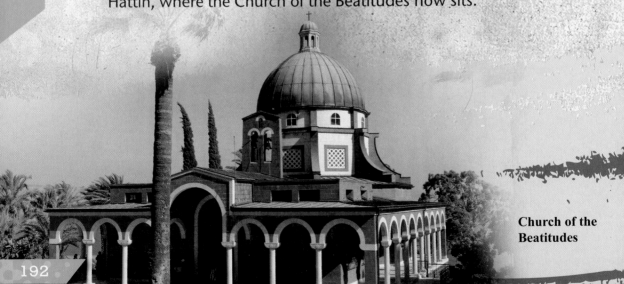

Church of the Beatitudes

DID YOU KNOW?

Beatitudes
(bee-at-te-toods)
are God's blessings.

TEACHING, THE OLD wAY

Teachers today spend a lot of time on their feet. But in the days of Jesus, both the rabbi (the Hebrew word for "teacher") and the students sat during the lessons. There were no school buildings. Lessons could be given outdoors, or in a person's house, or in a Jewish place of worship called a synagogue. Jesus even taught while sitting in a boat!

Famous Sayings from the Mountain

If some of the things Jesus said on the mountain seemed familiar to you, they should. People still use some form of those sayings. For example:

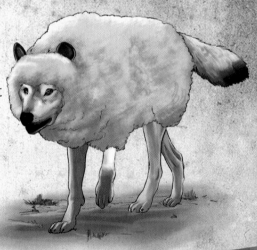

- "A wolf in sheep's clothing" is a way to say that someone is hiding their bad intentions under the appearance of kindliness.
- "Turn the other cheek" means to turn away, or not strike back, when someone harms you in any way.
- "Casting pearls before swine" means wasting something good on someone who can't appreciate it.
- "Hiding your light under a bushel (or basket)" means not letting people see the good things you do.

Let it Shine, Let it Shine

You may have sung the song "This Little Light of Mine, I'm gonna let it shine." The second verse starts: "Hide it under a bushel? No!" The song is based on one of Jesus' teachings: "Make your light shine so that others will see the good you do."

The Storm
Matthew 8.23–27; Mark 4.35–41; Luke 8.22–25

People who saw Jesus heal the sick wondered, "Could Jesus be the Messiah? Could he be the one God has sent to save us? Is he really the Son of God?" But when they heard about these miracles, the people said, "It must be true. Who else could do these things?"

Jesus called his disciples together. "Come, get into the boat and take me across the lake."

Jesus was tired. He lay down at the back of the boat and soon was fast asleep.

Peter kept glancing up at the clouds. By the time they reached the deepest part of the lake, the wind suddenly began to howl.

The disciples could no longer control the sail. The boat bounced wildly on the waves, which grew higher and higher. Water began to splash over the sides.

"We're going to sink!" James yelled.

The disciples turned to look at Jesus, who was still sleeping. John touched his arm and said, "Teacher, wake up! We are about to drown! Don't you care?"

Jesus opened his eyes. He stood up and turned to face the wind and said, "I command the winds and the waves to calm down."

In that instant, the wind stopped blowing and the lake was still.

"Why were you afraid?" Jesus asked the disciples. "Don't you have any faith?"

Now the disciples were more afraid than they had been during the storm.

"Who or what is this man?" they asked each other. "Even the wind and the waves obey him!"

Loaves and Fish for Everyone
Matthew 14.13–21; Mark 6.30–44; Luke 9.10–17; John 6.1–14

Jesus and his disciples were in the village of Capernaum near the shore of Lake Galilee. They had been on the road for many days, visiting towns and villages and were very tired. Always, there were crowds of people eager to hear Jesus teach. Always, there were sick people. Jesus felt sorry for them and healed them all.

"Let's go to a place where we can be alone and get some rest," Jesus said.

"But look at this crowd," Peter said. "How can we get away from them?"

Jesus smiled and said, "This way." He pointed to the lake where their boat was waiting. "We will go to Bethsaida," he said. Immediately, the disciples and Jesus got in the boat and set sail.

Many people saw them leave and figured out where they were going.

The crowd turned around and headed toward the road that went to the village.

When Jesus and the disciples got to Bethsaida, they found the people already waiting for them.

"They are like sheep without a shepherd," Jesus said. "We must take care of them."

He led the people to a grassy hill. They sat down and listened for hours as Jesus taught them about God's kingdom and told many parables. It was almost evening, and Philip said to Jesus, "We should let these people leave so they can go to buy something to eat."

"You give them something to eat," Jesus said.

Philip looked puzzled. "What can we give them? We don't have any food."

"Nothing at all?" asked Jesus.

Andrew said, "I saw a boy with five loaves of bread and two fish in a basket. But what good would that do? There must be five thousand people here!"

Jesus told Andrew to bring the boy to him. He took the basket and held up one of the loaves, saying, "God, we thank you for this food."

The basket was passed around. Each person took some bread and fish. There was enough for everyone! There was even some left over. Jesus asked his disciples to gather the leftover food. They came back with twelve large baskets filled to the top!

Afterward, everyone talked about the miracle. Jesus had fed five thousand people with just five loaves of bread and two fish!

Jesus Walks on Water

Matthew 14.22–33; Mark 6.45–52; John 6.16–21

After the people had eaten, Jesus told his disciples, "You go back to the lake and get into the boat. I must send these people away now. Then I am going up to the top of the hill to pray. Don't wait for me, but return to Capernaum at once."

The disciples walked down the hill and got into the boat. They started back to Capernaum.

Jesus spent a long time on the hill. When he finished praying, he walked down and stood on the shore of the lake. A fierce wind had come up. When Jesus looked across the lake, he saw that the disciples were in trouble. The boat, halfway across the lake, was being tossed around in the rolling waters.

Jesus took a step into the lake. But instead of sinking into the water, Jesus stayed on the surface. He walked on top of the swirling waves toward the disciples.

On the boat, James looked across the water

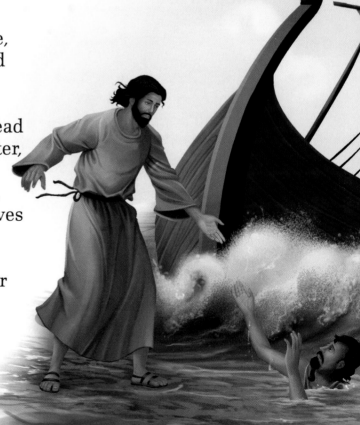

and cried out, "Look there! What can this be?"

The others saw Jesus, his robes blowing around him in the wind. They started to shake with fear. "It's a ghost!" they yelled and huddled together.

Then they saw that the figure was not a ghost.

Jesus came close to the boat and said, "Don't worry. I am Jesus. You should not be afraid."

But Peter could not believe his eyes and ears. He replied, "Lord, if it is really you, tell me to get out of the boat and walk over to you."

Jesus held out his hand. "Come," he told Peter.

The wind was blowing even harder now, and Peter got up, his heart beating so fast he could hardly breathe. Slowly, Peter got out of the boat. He put his feet on the water and took a step or two. But when Peter saw how hard the wind was blowing, he was afraid. In the next instant, the waves grabbed him, and he started to sink.

"Save me, Lord!" he shouted. Right away, Jesus reached out his hand and lifted Peter up.

"You don't have much faith. Why do you doubt?"

The moment Peter and Jesus got into the boat, the wind died down, and the water was calm again.

The disciples looked with wonder at Jesus. "You really are the Son of God," Peter said.

And they all knelt down and worshiped him.

Lazarus
John 11.17–43

One day, a man came running up to Jesus. "Master!" the man cried. "You must come with me. Your friend Lazarus is very sick. His sisters beg you to go and heal him."

Jesus told the man, "My friend's sickness won't end in death. It will bring glory to God and his Son."

Jesus loved Lazarus and his sisters, Mary and Martha, but he didn't rush off right away. He waited two more days.

When Jesus went to the house in Bethany, he found many people there. They had come from Jerusalem to comfort Mary and Martha. Lazarus had died four days earlier.

Martha ran up to Jesus.

"Lord," Martha said, "you are too late. If you had come sooner, my brother would not have died."

Jesus told her, "Martha, your brother will live again. Anyone who has faith in me will never really die. Do you believe this?"

"Yes, Lord!" she said. "I believe you are the Son of God. You are the one we hoped would come into this world." After Martha said this, she went and privately said to her sister, Mary, "Jesus is here, and he wants to see you." The sisters led Jesus to the tomb where Lazarus was buried. A large stone had been put at the entrance of the tomb. Jesus told the people to roll the stone away.

"But Lord," Martha said, "you know that Lazarus has been dead for four days."

Jesus replied, "Didn't I tell you that if you had faith, you would see the glory of God?"

Everyone watched as the stone was rolled aside. Jesus looked up toward heaven and prayed. "Father, I know you always answer my prayers, but I am saying this so that the people here will believe you sent me."

Then he turned to the tomb and shouted, "Lazarus, come out!"

There was silence as the people stared at the tomb. Then a cry went up, "I see him! Lazarus is alive!"

The man who had been dead came out. His hands and feet were still wrapped with strips of burial cloth.

Jesus then told the people, "Untie him and let him go."

Think about it...

What gave Jesus the power to do these miracles? How do you think they helped the people believe in him as the Son of God?

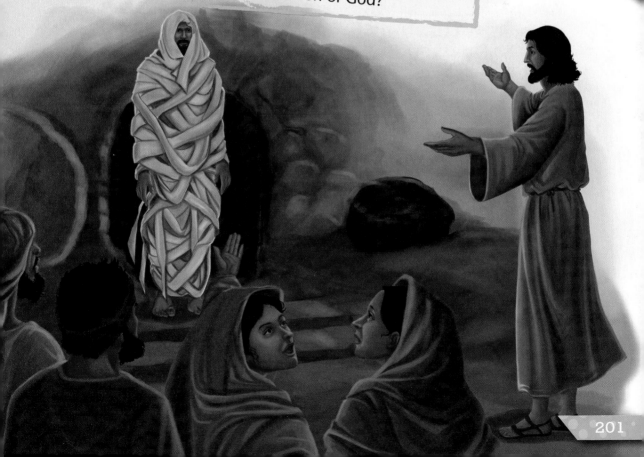

All About Jesus and Miracles

Five Thousand Meals

When Jesus fed the crowd, he turned a
few loaves of bread into enough to feed
5,000 people. What if you had to buy all that
bread today? Find out how much a loaf of bread costs—
then multiply that by 5,000. That's a lot of dough! A helping
of fish for each person could add three times as much to the bill.

The Tomb of Lazarus?

Today, people flock to the village of el-Eizariya on the West
Bank to see a tomb that is believed to be that of Lazarus. The
town, which means "Place of Lazarus" in English, is on the site
of the biblical village of Bethany. The tomb was discovered
about 1700 years ago, but there is no proof it is the actual
place where Lazarus was buried.

Burial Customs

During the time of Jesus, women were in charge of preparing the dead for burial. First they washed the body. Then they smoothed on a mixture of spices, oils, or perfume. Finally, the body was wrapped in strips of cloth. Lazarus came out of his tomb with the cloth still covering him.

DID YOU KNOW?

Forty of Jesus' miracles are noted in the Bible.

Having faith

Have you ever heard the expression, "O ye of little faith?" This comes from old versions of the story, "The Storm," in the book of Matthew. People say this when they are sure they can succeed at something that others doubt can be done.

DEAD OR ALIVE?

There are stories about people whose hearts stop beating but who then come back to life a few minutes later. Doctors call this the "Lazarus syndrome." No one knows for sure what causes the experience. It is extremely rare.

Who were Mary and Martha?

These sisters were two of Jesus' best friends. He and his disciples often went to their house when they were going to or from Jerusalem. During one of these visits, Mary showed her love for Jesus in a special way. She poured perfume on his feet and then dried them with her long hair.

Perfume jars may have been made of clay or glass.

Jesus in Jerusalem

Matthew 21.1–17; Mark 11.1–11; Luke 19.28–48; John 12.12–19

The people of Jerusalem greet Jesus with cheers. But he has enemies who are afraid he's becoming too popular.

"Clear the road! Clear the road!" Thousands of voices chanted. "Jesus is coming! Clear the road."

The people of Jerusalem had been waiting for hours. They knew that Jesus would be coming to the city for Passover, and the holiday was only a few days away. Jesus and his disciples had just been spotted up ahead.

In Jerusalem, no one had seen them for many weeks.

After Jesus had raised Lazarus from the dead, the chief priests were more worried than ever. To them, Jesus was a danger to the nation of Israel. He was leading the people away from the old teachings. There was only one way to stop him: he must be killed.

Jesus heard about the plot and left the city. He and his disciples had been hiding in a place near a desert far from Jerusalem. But now it was time for him to return.

The crowd moved back to clear the way. They placed palm branches in the middle of the road. This was the way to welcome important people to the city. Of course, there was no one as important to them as Jesus, the miracle worker. They believed he was the Messiah that God had promised to send into the world.

The voices got louder as Jesus passed before them.

"Hooray for the Son of David! God bless the one who comes in the name of the Lord! Hooray for God in heaven above."

Jesus smiled to see so many followers welcoming him to Jerusalem. But not everyone in the crowd was glad to see him.

One of the priests yelled out above the noise of the crowd, "Teacher, make these people stop shouting!"

Jesus replied, "What good would that do? If they didn't yell, the stones on the ground would start shouting instead."

After passing the gates of the city, Jesus got off the donkey. "Here, Peter," he said to one of his disciples. "Take the animal to a shady place and give it some water. The rest of you, go find something to eat."

The disciples left, and Jesus started walking toward the temple, the holiest and most important place in the whole country.

When Jesus got close to the temple, he stopped in his tracks. The courtyard looked like a marketplace, with cages holding sheep, cattle, and birds. People buying and selling were swarming like bees in a beehive. Along the sides, moneychangers had set up tables and were exchanging foreign coins for those needed in the temple.

Anger boiled up in Jesus' heart. He ran into the courtyard and went up to one of the moneychangers.

"This is a place of worship!" he shouted. He lifted the table and threw it to the ground. Coins rolled all over the floor. Then he went around to all the tables and flipped them over.

He turned to the stunned crowd. "This is a place of worship for all nations! But you have made it into a place of business where the moneychangers can rob you!"

The people who knew about Jesus were frightened to see him act this way. Others were ashamed of themselves.

The chief priests and other temple officials were more angry with Jesus than ever. They made money selling and buying at the temple. Who was Jesus to tell them what they should or shouldn't do? Why was he trying to change the way the people lived?

Every day crowds filled the courtyard of the temple to hear Jesus. The priests were discouraged. "There is nothing we can do!" they admitted. "Soon, everyone in the world will be following Jesus."

Think about it...

What was different about Jesus in this story? Did anyone ever make you angry because they showed disrespect for something you cared about? What did you do?

All About
Jesus in Jerusalem

A Hero's Welcome

Today, we speak of "rolling out the red carpet" when someone special comes to town. Sometimes, an actual red carpet is put down on the steps or the entrance of a building. We could say that Jesus was given the "red carpet treatment" by the people of Jerusalem, but instead of a carpet, they used clothing and branches of palm trees. Some people still use palm branches to celebrate Palm Sunday.

DID YOU KNOW?

Still Standing

About 70 years after Jesus died, the Romans destroyed Jerusalem's temple. A section of a stone wall is all that remains. Ever since the destruction of the temple, Jews have been visiting the wall in Jerusalem, mourning the loss of the temple. Because of this, the wall is known as the Wailing Place or the Wailing Wall.

Jesus in the Temple— the First Time

Jesus was 12 years old the first time he visited the temple. He had gone with Mary and Joseph to Jerusalem for the Passover holiday. Jesus liked talking with the teachers in the temple. He was still there when his parents returned home to Nazareth. They rushed back as soon as they noticed he wasn't with them. Jesus was surprised they had been worried. "Did you not know I must be in my Father's house?" he asked.

What is Passover? See page 75

WHAT DID MONEYCHANGERS DO?

At that time in Jerusalem, people used many different kinds of money, such as Greek coins and Roman coins. But when Jewish people wanted to buy something in the temple, they had to use special temple coins. The moneychangers were like bankers. They set up tables and gave the Jewish buyers temple coins in exchange for other money. Some moneychangers cheated and gave the buyer fewer temple coins than the other money was worth.

No Ordinary Palm Tree

Judea was famous for its date palm trees, which grew in forests all along the Jordan River Valley. In fact, these trees were known as Judean Date Palms and were the symbol of the kingdom of Judea. They could grow 80 feet tall, and their fruit was said to be sweeter and juicier than most dates. Although date palms still grow in the area, the Judean palms were wiped out more than 1,500 years ago.

The Easter Story

Passover

Matthew 26.17–30, 47–55; Mark 14.12–26, 43–50;
Luke 22.7–23, 47–53; John 13.21–30; 18.3–12

Jesus' enemies capture him. He is put on trial and sentenced to die on the cross. Three days later, God brings him back to life to show God's promise of life over sin and death.

It was the first day of Passover. Jesus knew that soon his enemies would come for him, so he chose a secret place to have the Passover meal with his disciples. He sent John and Peter ahead to prepare the supper.

Soon, Jesus and the other disciples were climbing the stairs to the room at the top of the house Jesus had chosen. They had just started to eat when Jesus said, "My friends, I have very much wanted to eat this Passover meal with you. I will not have another until I am in God's kingdom."

"What do you mean?" Peter asked. "Surely, you are not going to die."

Jesus replied, "Everything has already been decided. One of you is going to hand me over to my enemies. I will die, but, after three days, God will bring me back to life."

The twelve disciples were shocked. They couldn't believe what they were hearing.

"Who is it?" Andrew asked. "Who among us is the traitor?"

Jesus answered, "I will dip this piece of bread in the

sauce and give it to the one I am talking about."

He dipped the bread in the sauce and handed it to Judas Iscariot. He said to Judas, "Go and do what you have to do."

Judas looked at Jesus for a moment and then ran out of the room.

Later, Jesus and the other disciples went to the Mount of Olives as they usually did after the Passover meal.

Jesus went to walk in a garden to pray. The disciples went to sleep. When Jesus came back, the disciples were still asleep.

"Get up!" he said. "The one who will betray me is already here!"

Just then, a large mob of men with swords and clubs came over the hill. Some of the priests from the temple were with them—so was Judas Iscariot. He was carrying a sack filled with money. The priests had given him thirty pieces of silver to lead them to Jesus.

The men surrounded Jesus and grabbed him.

Jesus said to them, "Why didn't you arrest me before when I was at the temple?" Then he answered the question himself. "I tell you all this happened so that what the prophets wrote would come true."

The men sneered at him. "You think you are the Messiah, the Son of God? You are nothing but a criminal!" And they took him away.

Jesus on Trial

Matthew 27.11–26; Mark 15.2–15; Luke 23.13–25; John 18.33–40

The priests and temple leaders had finally found a way to get rid of Jesus. They had told the Roman governor that Jesus was bragging that he was more powerful than the Emperor. After all, wasn't he telling everyone that he was a king?

Jesus stood before the governor, Pontius Pilate.

"What do you have to say for yourself?" the governor asked Jesus. "Are you really the King of the Jews?"

Jesus said, "Those are your words!"

Pontius Pilate didn't know what to do. He was sure that Jesus wasn't guilty of any crime, but the priests were very powerful men. They could become dangerous enemies as well.

Then Pilate had an idea. Every Passover, the governor let the people choose one prisoner to be set free. He turned to the crowd standing outside the courtyard.

"Which prisoner do you want me to set free—this man, Jesus, or the one named Barabbas?" Now, the governor knew that Barabbas was a terrorist and murderer. He thought the people would free Jesus. But the priests and temple leaders had gone through the crowd and told them what to say.

"Give us Barabbas!" they shouted.

"And what should I do with Jesus?" the governor asked.

"Execute him! Nail him to the cross!"

Now I have no choice, thought Pilate.

He asked for a bowl of water and washed his hands so everyone could see. He said to the crowd, "I won't have anything to do with this. You are the ones doing it!"

Then Pilate set the murderer, Barabbas, free. He ordered his soldiers to take Jesus to Golgotha—the hill where common criminals were executed.

Jesus Gives Up His Life
**Matthew 27.27–54; Mark 15.16–41; Luke 23.26–49;
John 19.2,3, 17–30**

Before they took him to Golgotha, the soldiers decided to make fun of their prisoner.

"So, you are the King of the Jews," one of the guards said. "Well, you need a king's crown and robe."

They put a red robe around Jesus' shoulders. They made a crown out of sharp thorn needles and put it on his head. Then some of the soldiers knelt down and pretended to worship him while the others laughed. Jesus stood silently.

Finally, the soldiers got tired of their joke. They took off the robe and crown and led Jesus to the top of Golgotha. There, they nailed him to a heavy wooden cross and raised it up between the crosses of two other men.

Jesus was in terrible pain, but he looked down at the soldiers and called out, "Father, forgive these people! They don't know what they are doing."

The criminals on the other crosses heard him.

One said angrily, "They say you are the Messiah. Why don't you save yourself and save us!"

But the second man shouted back at him. "Aren't you afraid of God? We are guilty, and we got what was coming to us. This man didn't do anything." Then he said to Jesus, "Remember me when you come into power!"

Jesus replied, "I promise that today you will be with me in paradise."

The minutes crawled by, and the men on the crosses became silent and still. Around noon, a strange thing happened at Golgotha—the sky suddenly turned dark. "What's happening?" the soldiers asked each other. "There are no clouds, but the sun has stopped shining!"

The sky stayed dark for three hours. Then Jesus called out, "Father, I put myself in your hands!" And he died.

One Roman officer standing near the cross saw how Jesus died. Suddenly, he felt a great sadness and said, "This man really was the Son of God!"

Some of Jesus' close friends had watched the terrible sight from a distance. They bowed their heads and cried. Their hearts were broken.

Jesus Is Alive
Matthew 27.57–66; 28.1–20

The body of Jesus was taken down from the cross and wrapped in fine linen cloth. His friends carried it to a tomb that had been cut from solid rock.

Some women from Galilee were at the tomb. Usually, they would rub perfume and spices on a body before it was buried. But it was already the evening before the Sabbath and according to Jewish law, no work could be done.

The men rolled a big stone against the opening. The women would come back after the Sabbath to perform the rites of burial.

Very early on Sunday morning, Mary Magdalene; Mary, the mother of James; Joanna, and some other women set out for the tomb. They were carrying jars of spices and perfume.

"Didn't you see that heavy stone they put against the opening of the tomb?" Joanna asked. "How will we roll it away?"

"Perhaps some of the men will be there," said Mary Magdalene.

But when the women got to the tomb, the ground began to shake. It shook so hard that the stone rolled away. Then the Lord's angel appeared and sat on it. The women stepped back, trembling.

The angel said, "Don't be afraid! I know you are looking for Jesus, but he isn't here. God has raised him to life, just as Jesus said he would. Go and tell his disciples."

The women ran from the tomb to find the disciples and tell them the joyful news. Along the road, they saw a man walking in the other direction. It was Jesus! They dropped to their knees to worship him.

He told them, "Go find the disciples in Galilee and

tell them to go to the mountain where I said I would meet them. I will see them there."

A short time later, Peter, Andrew, John, and the eight other disciples saw Jesus walking up the mountain toward them. He truly was alive! At last they understood everything he had been telling them.

"Go to the people of all nations and make them my disciples. Teach them to do everything I have told you. I will be with you always, even until the end of the world."

Think about it...

Every year we remember the death and resurrection of Jesus at Easter time. How would you have felt if you had been at the tomb on Easter Sunday?

A Brave Friend

The tomb where Jesus was buried belonged to a rich man named Joseph from the village of Arimathea. Joseph was a leader in the Jewish council, but he had believed in Jesus and his message about God's kingdom. After Jesus died, Joseph had the body taken to the tomb he had chosen for himself for burial. Joseph knew this could get him in trouble with the council, but he didn't care. His love for Jesus was more important than what the other council members would think of him.

WASHING YOUR HANDS

When someone today uses the phrase "I wash my hands of this," what they really mean is "don't blame me, I'm not responsible."

A Famous Painting

You can find it on mouse pads, mirrors, place mats, and even dinner plates. Leonardo da Vinci's painting, "The Last Supper," is probably the most famous painting in the world. The original can be seen on a wall in a convent in Italy. Da Vinci began working on the painting in 1495. It took him three years to finish it.

This is a copy of the Da Vinci painting.

What is Passover?
See page 75

The New Apostle

Jesus had chosen twelve men to be his apostles—men who would continue the work of Jesus. Now the eleven apostles needed to choose someone to take the place of Judas. Two men seemed to be good choices—Justus and Matthias. The apostles prayed that God would guide them to the right man. The man turned out to be Matthias.

What happened to Judas Iscariot?

When Judas found out that Jesus had been sentenced to die, he tried to give the thirty pieces of silver back to the priests. They wouldn't take it. Judas could not live with himself. He threw the money into the temple and went out and hanged himself from a tree.

The Garden of Gethsemane

At the foot of the Mount of Olives is the Garden of Gethsemane where Jesus was arrested. Gethsemane, which means "olive press," was the place where olives were crushed to get the fruity oil.

About American Bible Society

Mission
The mission of American Bible Society is to make the Bible available to every person in a language and format each can understand and afford, so all people may experience its life-changing message.

At A Glance
After almost 200 years of ongoing ministry, American Bible Society invites people to experience the life-changing message of the Bible. Offering an increasing range of innovative ministries to address core life questions and struggles, the Bible Society partners with Christian churches and national Bible societies to share God's Word both in the United States and around the globe.

Serving Today's Generations
American Bible Society brings the love of Jesus Christ and the life-changing message of the Bible where it's needed most. We challenge the notion that the Bible is a dusty, outdated rulebook. By serving today's generations, we provide anytime, anywhere Scripture resources where translation is lacking, access is blocked, crisis is present and life doesn't make sense.

Find out more:
AmericanBible.org

Additional Rescources:
American Bible Society offers Bible resources to introduce your children to Jesus' life and teachings. From toddlers to teens, you'll find the right Bible and other Bible-based materials geared for children at: Bibles.com